BRUSH ARBOR BIRTHRIGHT

Lou Ella Vaughn

To Virgie and Effie Collins
With fond memories
Lou Ella Vaughn

Gospel Publishing House/Springfield, Mo. 65802

02-0483

Library of Congress Catalog Card Number 86-80089
International Standard Book Number 0-88243-483-7

Printed in the United States of America

To the memory of Manerva

Virgil & Effie Collins
May the Joy of Heaven
Be Their Everlasting
Peace & Happiness
Rev & Mrs B H Givens

Contents

Foreword

Ben and Manerva Givens are typical of the stalwart individuals who pioneered a message which produced the wonderful heritage we enjoy today in the Pentecostal movement. This account is a thrilling story of the committed lives of two very special servants God called from a life of sin and despair, molding them into shining trophies of His grace and power.

This is a very human story that reflects the mountaintops and the valleys that are part of life for all of us. It deals with joys and sorrows, courage and tenacity. Through the entire narrative runs an inspiring cord of strong faith in God, which typifies the lives and ministry of these two dear servants of the Lord.

It was my privilege to closely associate with the Givens. I served as a contemporary in ministry, pastoring a church in the same region of Northern California where so much of their fruitful ministry was centered. I know personally many of the people who were blessed by their lives and ministry, several of whom are now also ministers of the gospel. The Givens became a dynamic force, used by God to change the course of thousands of human lives over the years. They saw duplicated in multiplied numbers of lost people the same transforming power of God that so radically changed their own lives.

I think preachers and their wives will particularly enjoy reading this book because it relates to many common experiences and emotions. At the same time it also bears a message for any Christian who will invest the time to read its pages.

Brother Ben Givens and his wife, Manerva, are the kind of people of whom we are proud. They are representative of a large segment of the early pioneers who blazed the trail of the Assemblies of God across America and throughout the world. With little formal education but a clear call of God upon their lives, they faithfully followed that call wherever it summoned them to minister. With the help of the Holy Spirit, they became self-educated, capable teachers and preachers of Christian doctrine. Many of our powerful old-time preachers were carved by the Spirit of God from the same rough timber as were Ben and Manerva.

This book reflects the true ideal of Christian ministry. It should serve as a pattern for the sincere servant of the Lord. Not seeking their own, but the welfare of other people, Ben and Manerva in turn saw their own lives blessed and enriched with heaven's peace and joy.

ROBERT W. PIRTLE
NATIONAL DIRECTOR
DIVISION OF HOME MISSIONS
ASSEMBLIES OF GOD

Introduction

The Pentecostal movement began early in the twentieth century in modest surroundings: abandoned schoolhouses, brush arbors, old storefronts—whatever was available and cheap. Even so, it was to become the fastest-growing religious body in the world.

What kind of people would occupy drafty warehouses or settle for a simple brush arbor shelter to preach the gospel to anyone who would listen? Who were these preachers of the "full gospel"?

They were the receivers of the outpouring of God's Spirit. They had been seekers after God's blessing in places such as Charles F. Parham's Bethel College in Topeka, Kansas, where on January 1, 1901, many of the students received the baptism in the Holy Spirit and spoke in unknown tongues. This marked the beginning of the twentieth-century Pentecostal movement. It spread to Houston, and from there to Los Angeles, taken by a black holiness preacher, William J. Seymore. For three years, beginning in 1906, revival continued there day and night, often around the clock. In this setting many were called to spread the good news.

And spread the news they did! Scores left with little more than a Bible, a spirit of sacrifice, and a burning message that Jesus is coming soon. Often they subsisted on flour and water or whatever they could find. They slept anywhere—on park benches, in barns, in schoolhouses, under bridges, on dry river bottoms, on beaches, in tents, on wagon beds, in open fields, and, sometimes, in jail. Often they slept in the place where they were holding services. But usually they didn't stay in one place very long.

All suffered privation; some, extreme poverty. If they had any money they usually gave it to someone in need and trusted God for their next meal. This spirit of unselfishness and compassion won many souls. But others were not receptive and often the preachers faced hostility and persecution. Disorganization, rejection by traditional churches, and lack of material resources forced the Pentecostals to organize. Great leaders emerged between 1910 and 1920, establishing the various denominations within the Pentecostal movement: people such as J. Roswell Flower, Joseph H. King, S. H. Argue, E. S. Williams, Thomas Ball Barratt, Frank Bartleman, Aimee Semple McPherson. They, along with scores of others, will be remembered as instrumental to a strong beginning.

But what about the second-generation Pentecostal preachers and leaders? They were the generation that stabilized the movement. These leaders moved the Pentecostals from brush arbors and storefronts into church buildings, managing at the same time to preserve much of the naturalness of their worship. They were the ones who settled into pastorates, teaching Christian doctrine and modeling spiritual maturity for their newborn congregations.

Of them, one of the most distinguished couples is Reverend and Mrs. Benjamin Henry Givens. Two weeks after our wedding on July 5, 1946, my husband and I left our home and families and traveled two thousand miles to Live Oak, California, where Reverend and Mrs. Givens were pastoring. Our first Sunday in Live Oak was a mixture of excitement, fear, and homesickness. As we hesitated near the entry of the church, the Givens immediately spotted us. They hurried down the aisle with the friendliest smiles I had ever seen and took our hands. They hugged us and said, "We're the pastors, Brother and Sister Givens. We're so glad you're here. We've already heard about you."

Our first letter home reassured my family that we were attending church. I told them that the pastors reminded me of Reverend and Mrs. G. E. Chambers, our beloved pastors in Arkansas. That was the highest compliment I could bestow upon the Givens and the best way I could tell my parents that the Live Oak church had leaders who cared about their members, their community, but most of all cared about their calling from God.

I watched Ben and Manerva grow more beautiful with the years, never wavering in their relationship to God and their duty as His ministers. They spent sixty-three years together, fifty-eight in His service, before the Lord called Manerva home on November 19, 1982.

I have chosen Ben and Manerva Givens as representative of the many beloved pastors and leaders of a generation ago. Through their lives, typical, yet uniquely their own, I hope to show the young, and remind the old, of the love that existed and the Pentecostal unity these leaders helped develop, bringing us to where we are today. It is with great pride that I write their story.

1

A Bolt From the Blue

The entire Givens family had worked hard putting the brush arbor together after Ben was given permission from the school trustees to build it on school land. They found a place where they could work without cutting any large trees and began clearing out the smaller ones. Manerva helped Ben pull a seven-foot crosscut saw. Their little girls, Pauline, eight, and Maxine, six, raked and piled the brush to be put on top of the chicken wire stretched across the posts.

From time to time spring rains fell from the puffy white and dark clouds rolling in the sky and small rainbows would quickly appear and disappear. The cool rain and fresh smell of the clean air were welcomed. Pauline and Maxine would squeal with excitement and run for shelter, catching each other, kicking their bare feet, tumbling, and doing summersaults.

After the arbor was completed, the Givens family gathered scrap lumber from the mill in town, and wherever they could find any laying around, and made benches using tree trunks for the legs. They borrowed a truck and hauled sawdust for the floor. Ben made an altar from the longest and best boards, which he had laid aside.

"Do we have an old cigar box around anywhere?" Ben asked.

"There's one I use for our papers and things. I've had it ever since you used to smoke. What do you want it for?"

"Just get it and you'll see."

Ben trimmed four small limbs and attached them to one end of a slim post for support. Then he tacked the cigar box to the other end. He stood it just behind the altar and hung a gasoline lantern above it. He stepped back and looked at it with deep pride.

"How do you like that for a pulpit?" he asked.

He put a lantern on a corner post and placed a gas torchlight on the other side. He grabbed Manerva and swung her around while the girls watched and giggled.

"To God be the glory!" he called out for all to hear.

The arbor could have been made of marble, with great Roman columns supporting it. Antique Persian rugs could have covered the floor instead of sawdust. Kings and dignitaries could have been their audience. Even then, the four members of the Ben Givens family could not have been prouder of each other than they were that moment.

As Reverend and Mrs. Benjamin H. Givens stepped into their first brush arbor—completed only that day—they knew this was a part of them, of their calling and life.

It was a late spring evening in 1929 in southcentral Missouri, near the rural community of Ira, sixteen miles from Lebanon, the Laclede county seat. The out-of-door atmosphere made them feel close to God. The arbor could not seat all the people, and some were sitting on the ground outside or in their wagons or truck beds. The scene reminded the Givens of the beautiful outside settings Jesus sought when He preached to the multitudes.

This was the beginning of a new life for the Givens family. Ben had preached for several weeks in the schoolhouse nearby. Many had accepted salvation and scores had received the baptism in the Holy Spirit—thirty-seven in one night. Now the crowd had outgrown the small building, forcing them to move.

While the girls hurried toward the front of the arbor and crowded into the first bench with other young children, their parents lingered a moment with the people. Ben gave the men a robust handshake and broad smile, "Hello there, young feller, glad you could come out tonight. Did you get all that cotton chopped?" His masculine voice filled the arbor with warmth and welcome. No attitude he possessed was more pronounced or more important than his ability to love, his capacity for compassion, his willingness to serve others, and his determination to serve God. Nothing, not even the deep sorrows and disappointments he was yet to face, would change this.

Manerva hugged the ladies and spoke with gentleness. Her pretty face was framed with dark hair carefully waved, then tucked into a small twist low on the back of her neck. Her deep blue eyes sparkled as she looked directly into the eyes of each one she greeted. Her effervescence complemented her beauty and virtue. "Hello, it's so good to see you tonight," she spoke to each one. "I'm so glad you got to come."

Weather-worn faces returned the infectious smiles. Some were excited and said, "We're glad to be here. Looking forward to a good service," or, "This arbor's better than the schoolhouse, more room and fresh air."

However, some took the Givens' hands but were cool and withdrawn. Ben and Manerva usually gave them an extra hug.

As the Givens moved among the people, working their way toward the front, the ladies eyed Manerva's meticulously-made clothes.

"Same as every night, fresh and clean, not a wrinkle no place," they whispered to each other.

"I never could iron that good, especially white broadcloth. It's hard to get the wrinkles out."

"Yes, and they won't stay out once you put it on, even if it is starched. I wonder how she does it. She must of stood up in the car all the way here."

The song leader had arrived from Lebanon just ahead of the Givens family. His cattle truck was filled with men. Two other trucks followed him also carrying several men. The song leader quickly went to the front and found two songbooks in the cigar box. He looked toward the entrance of the arbor and spotted the Givens.

"This all the songbooks you got?" he asked, quickly going to them.

"Yes," Ben replied. "I ordered them from Springfield for thirty-five cents apiece. I couldn't afford any more. I'm hoping I can order some more pretty soon."

"Well, guess this'll have to do. Everybody can probably follow along all right without books."

Ben did not know the gentleman but had been told that he was a good song leader. Earlier he had stopped by to look at the arbor, and Ben asked him if he would lead the singing that night.

He seemed surprised, but said, "Oh, I don't know. If I can, I'll be here early."

"I'm sure obliged to you for your help," Ben said.

The services began. The singing echoed across the

hills, ringing out sincere, innocent worship to God. They all clapped their hands, swayed their bodies, and raised their voices in adoration. They sang of the hope of a better place, of a beautiful mansion, and of a day of rejoicing when they would meet the Saviour.

But as Ben listened, the sound of the music began to give way to a pervading sense of warning from the Holy Spirit. *Something is wrong,* he thought. Quickly he surveyed the entire scene. *No one's disturbed.*

Yet a strange feeling seemed to pour over him like oil. He reached out and took Manerva's hand. It was cold and trembling. She also had been warned. They leaned toward each other and prayed, "Lord, we don't understand our fears, but You are in charge here, and we humbly ask in Jesus' name that You take care of the situation."

Suddenly lightning lit both sky and earth and a loud clap of thunder sounded directly above the arbor! It shook the place like an earthquake. Torrents of rain fell. People began to run, piling into the cattle trucks and other vehicles. Ben and Manerva grabbed their Bibles, lanterns, and songbooks, and called out to the girls to get in the car. By then it was loaded and the girls had to sit on top of everyone. Ben followed the trucks up to the schoolhouse and broke the lock. Everyone rushed in. They built a fire and began to dry their clothes.

Ben stood at the schoolhouse window and watched the lightning as it flashed. Then he looked out across the hills to the east, then south, then north, and saw only clear sky. He moved to the other side of the room and looked to the west, then south, then north, and again saw only clear sky. The cloud was directly over them and nowhere else! He began to weep before the Lord, not understanding it.

The next morning the Givens surveyed the damage to the brush arbor and found nothing destroyed. The day was clear and bright, and by early evening people began to gather for another service. Manerva started the song service. The song leader drove up with several men, and they moved into the arbor.

Ben's sermon was on the Prodigal Son who had strayed from his father's house but realized his mistake and come home. People began to weep and rush to the altar to ask forgiveness. The young song leader and his friends also made their way toward the front and began to cry. As Ben and Manerva knelt beside them the men raised their heads and asked the Givens for forgiveness.

The leader confessed, "Last night I was leading these men to get rid of this place. We wanted to do away with you holy roller preachers once and for all. After you asked me to lead singing we got together and decided that during the song service I would jump up like I was shouting before God, grab the lantern and throw it on top of the arbor so it would explode and start a fire. Then the other two lanterns would be throwed on top and explode. That thunder clap came just as I started to jump up. It proved to us that God has His hand on you, and that there's something to this whole thing."

Later Ben slipped away from the arbor and knelt alone. He looked back at the arbor for a moment and watched the crowd. Some milled around getting ready to leave. A few knelt alone while others prayed together at the altar. Some rejoiced. Some sobbed confessions of sins and guilt. Others talked and watched the activity at the same time. But all were illumined by the lanterns still hanging at the sides. Manerva stood in the midst of it all with arms outstretched toward heaven, her white dress glowing in the light, tears streaming down her face, as she rejoiced and praised God for His love and care.

2
Stepfather

Ben had never known love until Manerva. They first met in the spring of 1919. They were married six months later.

Before Manerva, hatred, loneliness, and rejection were Ben's constant companions. He was born April 2, 1894, in El Dorado, Kansas, to David and Jennie Matheny Givens. His brother, Leonard Edward, was three years older. He had a younger brother and sister.

A few months after his sister's birth in 1901, his father took the children in his arms and held them closely, tousling their hair, kissing each one. He told them to be good and mind their mother because he had to leave and wouldn't be back for a long time.

One of the many problems between David and Jennie Givens had been his desire to go to the Pentecostal meetings and see what they were all about. Jennie refused to go and wouldn't allow it discussed in the children's presence.

Jennie attended the Methodist church from time to time, but was a member of the local Baptist parish. The little she had heard about the holiness people and the Pentecostals with their demonstrations didn't agree with her idea of religion.

Jennie knew that those who left the church were

considered to be of lower class status, socially deprived, and ignorant. She wanted nothing to do with them and feared that in some way she might be linked with them. To her, conversion was a social rite that gave her acceptance into the circles of the church, the first step toward community status.

Ben never saw his father again. He soon forgot his kind face, soft words, and gentle touch. He didn't see the tears of a heartbroken man as he walked away. Ben couldn't remember the kind deeds his father had done. As a very young boy Ben began to blame his father for the bad things in his life.

Shortly after David left, Jennie married Frank Corbin. Frank's mother had told Jennie that as a young man he was a Christian, a musician in the church, and a Bible teacher. But he left home and for twenty-one years no one heard from him.

Frank and Jennie married shortly after he returned. Frank moved into their tiny two-room house and immediately set rigid rules of discipline for each child. His cruel, heartless attitude soon turned the children's lives into a nightmare of abuse and torture. He repeatedly cursed and beat them, leaving them, cold and hungry, to sleep in the barn. Often they were kept home from school to hide their stripes and bruises. Deathly fear gripped the family, including Jennie.

One day when Ben was thirteen years old, he stood with one hand clutching the half-open door of their tiny house, watching the gathering of the gray, late summer twilight and knew it was time to go. He picked up a red bandana, sagging with his few belongings tucked inside, and slowly tied its four corners together.

"You'll find Ed all right," his mother spoke, almost

a question. Her face was weary and her broad frame stooped under the weight of the two young girls she held in her arms, Ben's half sisters, Mary and Lulu Belle.

Ed, the oldest brother, had left home three years earlier. He first went south to Arkansas and worked for a veterinarian, then moved to Kansas City.

"Yeah, I'll find him all right," Ben called out as he put on his straw hat and pushed the door open.

Ben reached the railroad tracks, crouched in a high weedy area, and watched as the Cannon Ball Freight slid to a stop right on time in front of the tiny depot. He waited until the last groan of the cars signaled their stop. He spotted an open door and sprang like a young deer into an empty boxcar and huddled, trembling, in the darkest corner. It soon pulled out with another groan and carried Benjamin Henry Givens away forever from the only home he had ever known.

All night the train clattered along, stopping at small towns and villages, letting its steam out, groaning, and pulling out again. Ben felt that he was in the belly of a huge monster, rythmically chewing with noisy teeth, stopping to belch and then chewing some more. At each stop Ben huddled in the corner, fearing the monster would sense his presence and throw him off.

At last, early in the morning, the train stopped again. Ben heard people's voices and hustling about. *This must be Kansas City,* he thought. Slowly he crept to the door and waited. When no one was near, he jumped out and ran across the tracks until he was safely out of the switchyard.

As far as he could see, buildings filled his vision—a mountain made of buildings! Never had his eyes looked upon such a sight. Never had his mind conceived such a thing.

Ben drifted down the street smelling the scents of dirty saloons and tired grease. Hunger growled inside him and changed his fear into a peculiar kind of courage. "I'll get a job, and I'll find Ed."

All day he walked, asking anyone who would stop and talk to him where he could get a job and if they knew Ed. No one helped. Sometimes he would drop to the ground and rest until he could continue on.

"Mister, you know where I can get a job?" he asked again.

"No, sir, I'd like to have one myself."

Finally his question got an answer he could live with.

The man looked at Ben for a moment, then said, "Go down the street till you come to Fourteenth Street, go left till you hit Woodland, then go in the labor union building there on the corner. They might have something."

"Thanks, Mister, much obliged!" Ben started running before the man finished.

At the labor union a crowd of men milled around inside, talking and grumbling to each other. Ben had no idea why they were there. Finally, after brushing off his clothes, he took off his hat, ran his fingers through matted hair, and then pushed his way in.

"Mister, I'd like a job," he said to the first man who looked at him.

"Hey, everybody, this dirty kid wants a job," he called out.

The men turned and looked at Ben and laughed. "What's new, boy, we all want a job," they sneered.

"I'll do anything," Ben shouted back. "Are there any jobs anywhere?"

"Don't know of none," someone answered.

Ben had never heard of a labor union and didn't know what was happening. After a long wait he saw a man come in the door.

"I need someone to work in my yard putting down sod. I'll pay thirty cents an hour," he called out.

Ben leaped to his side and yelled, "I'll take it, Sir. But I've got to have something to eat before I can work."

A man with an English accent yelled, "Oh, no you don't, kid. You ain't going to work for no thirty cents an hour when union scale is thirty-five."

Ben didn't understand and ignored the man, "Mister, I'll work hard if you'll take me."

A circle formed, and they began yelling, "Get him, kid, get him, kid!"

Just then a voice from behind called out, "Don't touch that boy or there will be one less Englishman in Kansas City."

Disbelief filled Ben's body as he turned and saw the sweetest sight he had ever seen in his life—his brother Ed!

3
Riding the Rails

"I can't believe I found you in a labor temple. How in the world did you get there?" Ed asked after he pulled Ben away from the men and started toward his apartment. Ben sighed and walked close, very close, to Ed as he told him the events of the last few days.

They walked six blocks to 629 Woodland Avenue, and the door opened to a small apartment. Ben could only stare as his brother, just three years older than him, introduced a wife, Inez, and three small children.

Ed reached into a closet and handed Ben a pair of pants and a shirt. "Go down the hall to the bathroom and get out of those filthy clothes, scrub about an hour, put these on, then get back in here. Here's some soap and a towel. Now get!"

When Ben returned Ed had soup heating on the stove. "You don't look like you've eaten for a year," he said. "Eat this kinda slow then crawl in bed and sleep a while."

Many hours later Ben woke to see the morning sun coming through a small window. He sat up and saw his own overalls and shirt hanging over a chair, clean and ready to wear.

"Ed, when did you get married?" Ben asked as he dressed.

"Oh, not too long ago. She's that horse doctor's girl that I worked for in Arkansas."

"You didn't write us about it."

"I know. I don't know if it's going to work out. She's not what I thought. I didn't know she'd been in a reform school till after we married. The old doc sorta tricked me into it."

"Did she wash my clothes?"

"No, I'm getting pretty good at that kind of thing," Ed replied. Then he asked, "Mama all right?"

"If you call living with the devil himself all right, I guess she is." Ben's anger surfaced at the mention of Frank.

"Still that bad, huh?" Ed asked. "Things get worse after I left?"

"How could they get worse? I guess he could have killed one of us, but he wouldn't risk his own hide doing that."

"I'm afraid he'll kill Mama," Ed said.

That hadn't occurred to Ben. "He wouldn't do that, would he? She sure is afraid of him. You don't really think he would, do you?"

"Stop worrying, Ben. Mama can pretty well take care of herself, you know. Now that we're both gone it might make a difference. Mama know you left?"

"Yes. She got me a minor's work release and told me to go see if you could help me find some work."

The two brothers sat quietly drinking coffee, deep in their own thoughts.

Ben broke the silence, "I ain't never going back, not ever, even if I don't see none of them again. I ain't going to get beat up or kicked ever again." His teeth clenched. "I hate Frank Corbin's guts. I hate our own dad, too. I hope they both rot in hell." Tears were streaming down his face.

"You're the one that's rotting. Hate's rotting out your insides. What's Dad got to do with it anyway?" Ed asked.

"He could have stayed with us. You know, Ed, he could have stayed. It's really all his fault. He left all four of us and Mama and just went off to God knows where. She married Frank just so we'd not starve. Ha! Better starved than beat to death. I hate Dad maybe even more than I hate Frank."

"You don't know why Dad left. Maybe he had a reason. Besides, he never beat us with a strap."

"I don't care why Dad left. He just shouldn't have. Leaving us for Frank to beat was just the same as beating us himself."

Although Ed was still looking at his brother, he was seeing something else. "It sure was different when Dad was at home. Once, when I was real young—don't guess you remember—our neighbor had some little pigs and I liked to go up there and play with them. Every time I went they'd get out of the pen and I'd get in trouble. Dad talked till he was blue in the face, but I'd just go right back whenever I got the chance.

"One day the pigs got out again and our neighbor came down and told Dad. He made me go outside and cut a bunch of switches. Then he stood me in a chair and gave me the biggest switch. He said, 'Ed, now you're going to whip me, or I'm going to wear out these other switches on you.' I had to whip him till the blood ran down his back. I sure didn't let them pigs out anymore."

"I don't want to talk about him," Ben snapped.

"Well, we don't have to talk about either of them,

and we never have to go back," Ed answered. "We'll go to the union hall tomorrow, and I'll show your work release to the man I've been working for and see if he's got a job you can do. We will just forget everything and start out fresh."

The next day Ed's boss hired Ben to clean around new building sites. Ben worked hard and learned quickly. Soon he was helping Ed finish cement.

The unusually warm winter gave the boys good work days and a pay envelope with more money than Ben had seen in his short life. Thirty-five cents an hour soon added up to a king's purse.

In a few weeks Ed's wife and her children left. The boys moved into a boarding house.

Inescapably, Ben learned to drink, curse, gamble, smoke, and work like those around him. His hearty laughter, jokes, and one-liners soon walled in a gentle, lonely heart.

Late one day Ed looked at Ben and asked, "Why don't we get out of this town?"

"Where'd we go?" Ben asked.

"I don't know, maybe up north and do some farm work. Get out in the wide open spaces and breathe some fresh air."

With that Ben, 14, and Ed, 17, stepped into an empty boxcar hooked to a freight train that became a merry-go-round of freight trains and boxcars, going everywhere and nowhere. They ran from job to job for almost seven years.

One night as the boys slept under a bridge Ben wondered if he had ever belonged anywhere. He wondered if death wouldn't be better than life. It couldn't be worse. No one would miss him. No one wanted him. He was worthless. Was there no one who cared? Loneliness was a dull, unguided blade, sawing out his spirit, destroying him. He felt he was dying, not because he had lost someone, but because he had never had someone.

His thoughts drifted back home, to an incident a year before he had left. He had gone to church with his mother, and the sermon had so interested him that he memorized it almost word for word. Later he told his mother, "I can't get away from it."

Jennie took Ben over to the preacher's house that afternoon. Ben repeated the sermon.

"I've never heard anything like this," the man remarked. "Ben has a marvelous memory for the Word of God. I'd like to bring him into my house and help him. I wish I had a son like this lad. Maybe you would even let me adopt him."

Ben's mother made a choice that day, though she never put her decision into words; it seemed too trivial. She chose to ignore the entire incident.

Ben struggled to serve God for a while. He stopped cursing and fighting. But then he became the laughingstock of the school bullies. They taunted and beat him, trying to make him curse and fight them. He cried from the pain, and inside he was torn apart. His stepfather beat him each time he refused to fight, threatening to kill Ben if he didn't stop disgracing the family and fight back.

One day Ben did fight back, throwing a pumpkin in a bully's face. The boy ran home and told his mother, who came after Ben with a pitchfork. Ben ran, but Frank caught him and beat him. After that Ben quit seeking God.

As those memories haunted Ben, hate and despair blocked out all good. He did not dwell on God. Ben had turned his back on Him once; now he was sure God had forsaken him, like all the world had done.

If only I could change, he thought. *Someday, someway, somewhere, I will.*

But the changes didn't come.

Work was hard to find, but Ben and Ed picked up a job once in a while on farms or shoveling snow. Once they painted the inside of a saloon.

One day they walked to a café near the post office. Ben told Ed to wait while he went to see if their mother had written. As he walked up the post office steps his hands and face were blue and stiff against the December cold. His body shivered beneath his thin, worn coat.

An Army recruiting officer stood outside the post office door, warm and comfortable in his four-buckle overshoes and wool overcoat. Ben asked the recruiter, "Hey, Buddy, what would you take for that overcoat you got on? I'll trade you mine for it and throw in a little to boot."

The officer looked at Ben and said, "I don't know, hadn't thought about it. Come in my office and we'll talk."

Soon after that Ben was sworn into the United States Coast Artillery and ordered to Jefferson Barracks, Missouri. Ed also tried to enlist. But his eyes did not meet Army standards.

Through tears Ben told Ed he loved him, adding, "But my hobo life is over."

Ben Givens at 21, while he was in the United States Coast Artillery at Ft. Totten, New York

4

"A Mighty Cute Little Thing"

Two days after arriving at Jefferson Barracks, Missouri, Ben developed pneumonia and spent two weeks in the hospital. The day after he returned to the barracks an officer told everyone to pack and get ready to leave.

"Where are we going?" Ben asked, throwing things in his bag.

"We're being shipped out," someone replied.

"But I ain't had no training yet."

"Either line up or be locked up," the officer bellowed.

Ben fell in line and boarded the train for Ft. Totten, New York. He was assigned to the 135th Mine Setting Company, Coast Artillery, the highest branch of the service at that time. He had access to a large, comfortable brick building equipped with a recreation room, a pool room, and a dayroom supplied with books, magazines, stationery, and desks. After enrolling in the base school, Ben spent hours in the dayroom studying for his high school diploma. He also taught himself all the training he missed at Jefferson Barracks. He read manuals and observed, but asked as few questions as possible.

For the first time in his life Ben began to realize a sense of self-worth. He was no longer ashamed or embarrassed about himself. He looked like, acted like, and dressed like everyone around him. He was equal with his peers. Depression began to leave. Suicidal tendencies disappeared. The hate that had developed since his earliest remembrances buried itself deeper in his soul, seldom surfacing.

After five months Ben was transferred to Ft. Dupont, Delaware. They, in turn, sent him on detached service to Ft. Mott, New Jersey, to be the cook's helper for the fifty-seven men occupying the small fort. After a short time Ben became the head cook.

Around a year later Ben's mother wrote that she was confined to a wheelchair with arthritis. The seven dollars and fifty cents Ben sent to her each month did not cover the medical expenses.

Even though Ben had not completed his high school requirements and still felt that he needed the Army to help with the direction of his life, he asked for a dependency discharge, hoping to get a good paying job and send more money to his mother. In March 1917 Ben was discharged and found work at a railroad company.

In June General Pershing landed in France and the United States entered World War I. Ben, realizing he would soon be recalled, decided to visit his mother. He arrived in Tulsa, Oklahoma, where Jennie was living. He had sent enough money to her while he worked on the railroad to pay for proper treatment for her arthritis. He found her at work as a waitress.

In October Ed moved to Kansas. Ben decided to visit him. The two brothers hadn't seen each other for three years. They stayed together until Ben was drafted in March 1918 for one more year of Army life.

Ed wrote Ben that he had found the most wonderful woman in the world.

> Her name is Leora Mitchell, and she's from Ira, Missouri. I never met anyone like her. She comes from a nice family, too. They live just over the state line in Dewey, Oklahoma, working in the oil fields there. I think I'm finally ready to settle down. After we're married we're going down somewhere around there, maybe on to Pawhuska. I'm sure I can get work there in the oil fields.
>
> Leora's niece Manerva is a mighty cute little thing. She said the the only reason I'm marrying Leora is because she didn't see me first. She wanted to know if there were any other Givens boys as handsome as me. I told her "no" but mentioned you anyway. Even showed her your picture. She wants to meet you.

The war ended November 11, 1918. Ben was discharged on March 18, 1919. He rode the train to Pawhuska, Oklahoma, to visit his brother.

"Mama's moving down," Ed told Ben almost as soon as he stepped off the train.

"All of them coming?" Ben asked.

"Frank and the two girls are."

"Where are they going to stay after they get here?" Ben asked.

"I bought two lots out here where they're planning a town. Thought I'd build me a house on one and give the other one to Mama. They ought to be worth something when they get the town built. I think they aim to call it Pershing, after the general."

Ben went to work dressing tools for the Nash Tool Company, subcontractors for the Phillips Drilling Company. His shift was from noon to midnight for nine dollars a day. He hired a man to build his mother's house while Ed finished his own. Both houses were ready to move into when their mother arrived. Ben stayed in a bunkhouse nearby.

"Ben, I can't wait for you to meet Manerva," Leora said one day. "I know you're going to like her. She's a nice girl and a lot of fun. She's been wanting to meet you, too."

One day in April Manerva's father had to go to town to see Ed and asked if she wanted to ride along. Manerva dressed carefully in her finest dress knowing she would finally meet Ben. Ben liked Manerva right away, and they spent the whole night together talking.

Manerva Armilda Evertson was born in her Grandfather John Slaven's home in Ira, Missouri, on April 13, 1900. Her parents homesteaded on a farm near Ira. They taught her to love the farm and enjoy work. They taught her to sing and dance and fear nothing. She sang to the cows and chickens, and to her baby brothers and sisters who soon began to appear. She sang to the dishes as she stood on a box to wash them. Before she was "knee high to a jack rabbit" she knew every song and dance in the hills.

In 1919 the family moved to Big Heart (which would shortly be renamed Barnsdall), Oklahoma, about fifteen miles from Pershing. By this time Manerva had seven brothers and sisters: Frank, Lee, Joan, twins Lola and Lonnie, Alene, and Helen. Her father worked for Nash Welding Company on oil rigs located near Big Heart.

A few days after meeting Manerva, Ben said, "Manerva, I want to be frank with you. Of all the girls I've known I think you're the nicest, prettiest, sweetest lady I ever met. I'm very deeply touched by you. You have the happiest, friendliest personality of anyone I ever saw."

Then, without a car, fifteen miles was a considerable distance. They began corresponding and saw each other whenever they could.

In September Manerva told Ben she was going to Delaware, Oklahoma (almost sixty miles from Pershing), to visit her uncle Ed Slavens. The night before she left, she and her mother came to spend the night at Leora's.

Ben came home at midnight and he and Manerva sat in Ed's car and talked.

Ben cleared his throat and very seriously said, "Manerva, I'm looking for a real companion for life and I'm very particular. I want to tell you something. I don't know whether you consider me in any sense at all, but I have a feeling that your affection for me is about like mine is for you."

They continued talking until 3:30 in the morning when Ben said, "I want to ask you a question, and I know you know what it is. I want to get married. In my heart I've chosen you. I want to be as honest about this as I can. I'm six years older than you, you know that. I've not hidden anything from you."

"Ben, I think an awful lot of you."

"Well, is that the best you can do?"

She smiled.

Ben continued, "I'll be frank with you. I want you for my wife. I've loved you from the moment I first saw you. I think you're just exactly the answer to the cry of my soul. Will you marry me?"

Manerva looked at Ben, threw her arms around him and, for the first time, kissed him. She said, "I have the same feelings toward you. I know for sure that there is such a thing as love at first sight. You're the answer to my desires. Yes, I'll marry you."

They decided to marry shortly after her return

from Delaware. While Manerva was gone, Phillips offered Ben a job in Ranger, Texas, about midway between Abilene and Fort Worth. When Manerva returned from visiting her uncle, she and Ben made plans to move to Texas and be married there.

The morning after they arrived in Ranger they found a place to rent, moved in, and dressed to go to Eastland, the county seat, to get married.

Ben looked at his bride standing by his side repeating the marriage vows. Her blue suit, with the flowers he had bought pinned on her shoulder, accented her big blue eyes. He had never seen such beauty, purity, honesty, and sincerity. It was October 6, 1919. She was nineteen, and for sixty-three years, one month, and fourteen days she proved that he saw her exactly as she was.

5

"The Girls Will Call Someone Else Daddy!"

One month after Ben and Manerva moved to Ranger, Ben was told to go to a drilling site miles from their home. The morning Ben left, Manerva went to the window and raised the heavy quilt tacked over it. Through the condensation that quickly formed on the cold glass she could see Ben's body bent forward and head bowed as he trudged through the mud and rain, moving out of sight.

Manerva remembered their conversation just before he had left. "I don't like leaving you here alone. I don't like it at all." He regretted bringing his bride to such desolation. "We could leave, you know."

"Hush, Ben." Manerva touched his lips with her fingers. "You're making good money; we'd better stay. Don't worry about me. I'm not gonna sit around feeling sorry for myself. I'll keep busy somehow."

"I don't want you working in town at any cafés or hotels. It's dangerous. And besides I might lose you to one of them no-good bums hanging around."

"Ben!" Manerva put her hands on her hips and turned her face up to his.

"I'm sorry, Nervy, I shouldn't have said that."

"No, you shouldn't. Don't you know by now that I'm going to be hard to get rid of?"

The raindrops on the window brought Manerva's

thoughts back to the moment just before Ben disappeared over a small hill. She wiped the moisture from the window with her sleeve as Ben turned, waved, and blew a kiss.

Manerva continued to look out the window, her gaze held by the rows of tar paper houses looming black and ugly against the heavy gray sky. They stood like mud hens on a tule lake, waiting, miserable. Manerva shivered, dropped the quilt, and moved to the warm fire.

Originally a farm trade center of less than a thousand, Ranger itself sat crouched in mud, lonely and dazed by the oil rush that gave it no rest. The deluge of rain—it would be one of the wettest seasons on record—added to its misery. The streets agonized under the load of thousands where hundreds had once been. The once quiet, dignified farming community had grown to thirty thousand in less than two years. Familiar dry goods, grocery, and feed stores strained with the new population, giving room for tar paper saloons, brothels, and gambling houses. Tree-lined residential streets sunk in the mud, while white houses with picket fences became lost among the tents and shanties. Hotel rooms rented both day and night with no linen change. Lobby chairs rented by the hour.

Lawlessness and cruelty flourished. Men died at night and were hauled away in the morning. Huge horses, pulling long trains of wagons loaded with heavy machinery, often sank in the mud and drowned on main street.

In the midst of the swirling crowds, easy money, whiskey, prostitution, and lawlessness, the newlyweds struggled to build the kind of relationship they both wanted.

But Ben's drinking became heavier and heavier. Isolated and lonely at the well sites he found whiskey a companion and gambling a pastime. When he came home he and Manerva sought pleasure wherever they could find it.

Manerva took her free heart and happy song into the dance halls and found partners who could do the Charleston, fox-trot, or whatever was the craze of the moment. Ben hated to dance. He usually sat in the corner, pulled a flask of bootleg whiskey out of his hip pocket, and gambled with his buddies.

Jealousy ate at his soul when Manerva danced with the same partner more than once. He became more angry and belligerent with each swig of whiskey. They began arguing and accusing each other. They each grew stubborn and determined. They would pout, passionately apologize, then start over.

By July the mud of winter had turned to powdery dust. The course of traffic cycled the dirt roads into a cloud that rained dust on the summer green foliage, turning the landscape back to a wintry gray.

Manerva was expecting their first child and wanted to be near her mother. So Ben quit his job and sold their property, and they boarded a train back to Pershing. There he went to work with his father-in-law dressing tools for Phillips Drilling Company at nearby well sites.

On September 23, 1920, their first daughter, Pauline Margaret, was born. They remained near Pershing, moving often to new well sites and living in temporary housing. On January 4, 1923, a second daughter, Juanita Maxine, joined their family.

One of Ben's Army buddies, Frank Stanley Gleason, became superintendent of Phillips. Ben left the fields, and for forty dollars a month began working as an operator at the plant.

For the first time since their marriage the young couple settled into a real home. For seven dollars and fifty cents a month they rented a two-bedroom company house. It had a bath, electricity, and gas. They furnished it with carpets and used furniture, including a piano, washing machine, and sewing machine. Manerva made drapes for the living room windows and curtains and a bedspread for the girls' bedroom. She made priscilla curtains for the master bedroom and batiste curtains for the kitchen. They planted a vegetable garden in the backyard. Manerva planted flowers all around the house. Ben made swings and doll furniture for the girls.

There were fifty-two company houses located at the plant site a mile and a half from town. Ben and Manerva knew all their neighbors and were happier than they had ever been.

When Ben was sober he was a kind and loving man. He adored his wife and daughters and was proud of his home. Manerva loved and respected him. But Ben's sober moments became fewer and fewer. Prohibition forced him to make his own home brew. He shared this chore with his father-in-law. Manerva fought. Ben fought back. They began to spite each other. Manerva deliberately angered Ben by dancing with the same man at the dance halls, and Ben deliberately drank more and more.

Their marriage was sinking. Manerva tried pouring out the liquor. Ben cursed her. One day he brought home two cases of fresh brew. Manerva uncorked all of the bottles, letting the contents go flat. Ben tried picking wild grapes to make wine. After he put the juice into jugs to ferment, the fermenting caused the jugs to make a thumping sound. Each day Ben would ask Manerva if his jugs had started thumping.

One day a jug thumped. Manerva uncorked it and poured out about half of the wine and filled it with water. When Ben asked about the wine she said, "It thumped for a little while, then stopped." A few days later, more thumping. Manerva repeated the process. Soon all the wine ruined.

Ben cursed and pouted. Manerva quarreled and fought. Their marriage reached its lowest point. Everything Ben loved seemed lost. Manerva's dreams disappeared. She tried to get Ben to leave. He told her it was his house since it belonged to his boss and she should go. She said it was her home and she and the girls intended to stay. But life finally became unbearable for Manerva and she made a decision.

"Ben," she spoke with no question in her voice, "you have a choice to make. You must decide between your family and the bottle. If you continue to drink I'm leaving you, and the girls will call someone else Daddy!"

"It's do or die, huh, Nervy?"

"Yes."

He left the house and wandered alone for many hours.

"Manerva," he called when he entered the front door. "I've made a decision. I'll never get drunk again if you will stay away from the dance halls and not dance with other men."

Manerva put her arms around his neck and said, "I'll do anything to make things better."

Ben held her close and said, "Now, mind you, I didn't promise not to ever drink a little. I just said I'd not get drunk. I have to drink with my buddies, but I'll not get drunk."

Ben's promise was hard to keep. His body cried out for the satisfaction he had found in liquor since he was thirteen years old. It tormented him, held onto him, and wouldn't let go. He became angry, quarrelsome, and difficult. But his stubborn will and determination prevailed. He continued to limit his drinking. Manerva wanted to flee from it all and sing her songs and dance her dances somewhere else.

Their life changed some, but suspicion, doubt, and fear continued to mar their union. The future held little hope for them. They began to lose sight of their dreams.

6

A Kiss of Fire

"Ben, you are drunk!" exclaimed Manerva.

"No, I'm not! Will you just listen to me?"

" 'Listen'? Listen to what? You have to be drunk to tell me we're going to church tonight. Ben, I warned you about drinking and you promised—"

"Nervy, hush and let me talk. I'm not drunk. I'd like to be right now, but I'm not. And I'm not going to church to go to church. I'm going to see what kind of old bag my daddy used to run around with."

"What on earth are you talking about?"

"I'm trying real hard to tell you, but you won't listen."

"All right, I'll listen, but you're not making any sense."

"Well, I will if you'll just hear me out. Wilbur Adkins told me today that there's a revival meeting going on at the high school auditorium, and he's been going to it. Couple named Casey, Gus and Jessie, I think, doing the preaching. The woman does most of it. Anyway, Wilbur said that last night they talked about starting out preaching with a man named David Givens, traveled with him and his wife for a long time. He asked me if I knew anybody by that name. I said that was my daddy's name."

Manerva asked, "Do you believe it's him?"

"I don't know. I'd rather hear a cow bawl as to listen to a woman preacher. But we're going, so get the kids ready."

Ben sat on the back seat of the auditorium and watched as Manerva and the girls continued down the aisle to the front. *Don't want anybody seeing me with these holy rollers,* he thought.

When the music started Ben noticed a large man up front singing with the deepest bass voice he had ever heard. *What a crazy fool you are to hook up with this bunch of people! With that voice you could sing anywhere,* he thought.

Then the testimonies started. Ben wasn't familiar with this kind of church service and thought each woman that stood to talk was Jessie Casey. Finally the large man went to the pulpit and introduced the speaker. She had been sitting behind a piano, hidden from Ben's view. Jessie was a beautiful lady with long black hair and a glow on her face. After she made the altar call, while the people were still singing, she walked down the aisle straight to Ben. She reached out her hand and said, "How are you, young man?"

"Very well," Ben replied. "Are you Jessie Casey?"

"Yes, I am."

"Did you ever know my father?" Ben asked.

"Who is your father?"

"David Givens."

She looked stunned, then tears suddenly burst from her eyes. She looked at Ben and cried out, "Which one of the boys are you, Ed, Ben, or Abe?"

"I'm Ben," he said, then wondered, *What's going on? She knows our names as well as I do.*

Mrs. Casey ran to the platform, grabbed the large bass singer, whispered to him, and he came running back to Ben. Tears were streaming down his face. He looked straight into Ben's eyes and cried, "Little David."

"I'm Ben."

The man put his hands under Ben's arms, lifted him up, and kissed him on the mouth. He said, "I've seen your old daddy put himself in a room, lock the door, and refuse food for three days at a time, praying that God would save his children."

Ben couldn't believe what he was hearing. "You mean my daddy prayed for me?"

"He never missed a day praying for you. Oh, Ben, you just don't know. We love your daddy like he was our own kin. He helped us get started in the ministry. We owe him so much. We watched him suffer from loneliness and grief for his children. We prayed with him and suffered with him. He's bad sick with miner's TB now and won't live very much longer if God doesn't heal him. If you live to be a hundred you'll never know how much your father loves you and your brothers and sister."

Gus and Jessie had met David and his "new" family through their association with Charles F. Parham's Apostolic Faith Movement. They all sat under Parham's teachings at Bethel College in Topeka, Kansas, and later traveled together in the ministry.

"David taught Jessie and me just about everything we know," Gus said. "Just watching his life made me want to serve God with all that's in me. Even in his troubles and sadness I don't think I ever knew a friendlier, more peaceful, or happier man than David. He wrote lots of songs. They always had a kind of tongue-in-cheek humor, with the message of salvation coming through loud and clear."

Once more Gus Casey slipped his hands under Ben's

arms, lifted him up, and kissed him again on the mouth. Ben had never seen a man kiss another man in his life. He had never known love like that.

Ben's lips began to burn. He thought the man had oil and mustard on his lips. Ben found a drinking fountain and tried to get water to wash it off. The burning grew worse. By the time he reached home the burning had crawled down his throat like a volcanic eruption oozing down a mountainside.

He drank home brew, but that didn't help. Manerva made lemonade. That didn't help. He drank ice water and ate crushed ice. Nothing helped. Every time he swallowed the burning moved down.

It grew more intense, tormenting him day and night. About a week later Ben felt it drop, as if it had form and substance, into his stomach. For three more weeks hell burned inside him. He wanted to die. He hated everyone, fought with everyone, and almost left his family.

On Thursday, April 24, 1924, Manerva suggested that they go back to church. The Caseys had moved from the school auditorium to an abandoned pool hall in Pershing.

Ben yelled, "I'm not going! Besides, you know that Maxine's sick. She might have pneumonia, and we can't take her out."

"We can go by the drugstore and get some medicine, stay for church, then give it to her when we get home."

To Manerva's surprise, Ben finally agreed to go.

He sat in the back row and watched again as Manerva and the girls moved toward the front. Anger boiled within him. The burning felt like liquid fire.

When the lady began to preach, tears came in Ben's eyes. He didn't want anyone to see him cry, especially his buddies who knew how he drank, cursed, and feared nothing. But the tears kept coming. He was afraid to leave and afraid to sit still. Finally, Mrs. Casey said, "If anyone here is in trouble, grieved, torn in home, with problems you can't understand, Jesus will help you if you will come forward."

Ben rose from his seat, ran to the altar, and cried out, "My God, help me to find You!"

He fell at the altar and began to beg. He didn't know how to pray, he just begged for help. A cloud as black as crude settled over him. The darkness changed to gloom, threatening to suffocate him with hopelessness. He cried for relief and begged God to forgive him.

He raised his head to see a golden light appearing above him, descending through the darkness, growing brighter as it moved toward him. "Help! Help!" he cried out. The light seemed to explode the blackness.

Trembling began in his knees and moved upward. When it reached his burning stomach, the fire leaped out. The greatest joy he had ever known filled his entire body. He couldn't remain on his knees. He jumped up and began to leap and dance. He kissed everyone near him—man, woman, or child.

Then he spotted Manerva at the other end of the altar. He didn't know she had followed him. He ran to her; they fell into each other's arms, cried, and asked forgiveness. All their troubles were forgotten.

Finally at home, Ben and Manerva tucked the girls into bed, without Maxine's medicine, and slipped into their bed.

Just before they fell asleep Ben said, "Sweetheart, I went to that old pool hall many times before it closed—drinking, gambling, smoking, cussing, and telling dirty jokes—and went away thinking that's what fun is all about. But I learned tonight in that same spot what real joy is. It's having all those things emptied out of my heart and having it filled with love and God so wonderful and new I don't know how to explain it."

"I know, Honey," Manerva said. "I felt a wonderful feeling in my heart that God has such amazing things waiting for us to experience I can't hardly stand it."

"I don't want to ever let Him down."

"We won't, Ben, we can't. Not after what He's already done."

"You know what? God answered my daddy's prayers. Can you imagine that, him praying for me all the time I was hating him? That's really something!"

"Yes, that's really something."

The early morning sun broke through the window and stirred their restful sleep. Never had spring been so gentle. The calm south wind touched the new leaves on the trees. The fragrance of the lilacs drifted in. The jonquils sang a song of spring, and the green grass covered the winter mud. The patch of sun on the floor warmed their feet as they began a new life.

Ben and Manerva quietly walked into the girls' bedroom and discovered that Maxine's congestion had broken in the night and she was healed.

7

"Preacher! Preacher!"

Ben and Manerva hungered for the knowledge of God. Their first Bible, ordered from Montgomery Ward for two dollars and ninety-five cents, soon became worn from use. They studied and prayed before Ben went to work. Manerva studied and prayed while Ben worked. And Ben studied and prayed each evening into the early morning hours. They shared with each other everything they discovered.

They anticipated the joys of each new day. Even the air around them seemed lighter since the weight of sin had been lifted.

But Ben's mother had become furious when she learned her son had become Pentecostal like his father. She felt he had disgraced the entire family. At work Ben suddenly became a turncoat in the eyes of his friends. He had been a leader among them, willing to try anything, not afraid of anyone, and rightly called the orneriest one of the bunch. They had freely helped themselves to everything around the plant; no one ever bought gas or oil for his car.

Now Ben's coworkers stared in amazement at the sudden change in Ben. Not one believed it would last, and they all set out to bring him to his senses.

"If we don't knock some smarts into him he might tell what we've been doing. We've had it too good for too long. We don't want nobody checking up and giving us any trouble," they decided.

They worked on Ben's ego, his self-confidence, his pride, his dignity—anything that would destroy his feelings of self-worth. They tempted him with his past sins. The persecution began with the "smoke treatment"—one man sitting on either side of him blowing smoke in his face. That didn't work. They harassed, teased, and mimicked him. He didn't fight back. They drew mocking pictures of him praying. They put water in his gas tank.

Ben's witness never failed except in one area: He could not stop cursing. It was so much a part of his speech he cursed by rote. There was a rhythm and certain art to his speech pattern. He tried to stop but always failed.

One day the plant had to be completely shut down. Each department moved quickly to keep the pressure from building and blowing out all the gaskets. Ben discussed the procedure with his superintendent, Mr. McCully. Then he began to tell his crew exactly what to do. He got excited and started cursing.

"Preacher! Preacher! Preacher!" they mocked.

Ben moved out into the middle of them and got down on his knees. He raised his hands up and asked God to forgive him for not being able to stop cursing. He rose and went to his superintendent and took his hand.

"Mr. McCully," he said, "I want you to forgive me. And I want these fellows to forgive me. I don't want to cuss. God helped me to get away from booze; God helped me to get away from cigarettes; God helped me to get away from stealing gas and oil. God helped me to get away from all those things, and He helped me to hold still when the men tormented me. But I haven't had any help here yet, and somehow God told me to do this. I'm apologizing, 'cause I want to be a Christian more than anything else in the world."

The men became silent. Slowly they formed a line, dropped their eyes, and one by one shook hands with Ben. He was delivered forever from cursing. God helped Ben to show his friends that he wasn't afraid to pray in front of all of them. He had lived a life of sin before them; he would do the same with his Christian life, no matter how difficult.

The Caseys stayed in Pershing about thirty days after the Givens were saved. Just before they left, Gus said to Ben, "Your father will be so happy when he hears you are a Christian."

"I'd be ashamed to write," Ben confessed. "The only letter he ever got from me was right after I got out of the Army. It was a hateful letter. I cussed and said everything bad I could think of. I told him that when I was little he left me, and I was raised in a hellhole. I blamed it all on him—it was his fault. I abused him with every unkind word I could think of."

"I hope you can forgive him and get all that anger out of your heart," Gus said. "I can find out where he is if you want to contact him."

"I've already forgiven him, but I don't think I'll write, not just yet." Ben lowered his head as he spoke.

"I'll tell you what I'm going to do. I'll give you your Grandma Givens' address. She just lives down in Tulsa. You can get in touch with her whenever you decide you want to."

The little group of Christians kept the pool hall for Sunday school and services. Among them they had different religious backgrounds and claimed different beliefs, but unity prevailed nevertheless. They invited every visiting minister to preach. No one thought to ask what denomination the speaker represented. No one cared. The Word worked into their hearts like a healing balm, soothing the deep gashes of sin.

But much of the Givens' early growth in the Lord continued to come from personal experiences that tried their faith and got them into the Word.

Soon God began to speak to Ben about going into full-time ministry.

"But, Lord, I don't know anything about the Bible," he prayed. "I never heard of but one Bible school, and it's over in Enid. And I don't have money to go. Besides, Nervy would never go with me, and I can't go without her. I can't break up my home. If I just had someone to teach me a little, maybe it wouldn't be so hard to know what to do."

Late one afternoon Manerva heard a knock on the front door. She untied her apron, hung it on a nail by the stove, pushed her hair into place, and went to the door.

"You Mrs. Givens?"

Manerva looked into the face of a beautiful young lady who could hardly have been much older than herself.

"Yes, I am," she said.

"I'm Doreen Justus. Some friends told me you are Pentecostal people, so I've come to visit you."

Manerva reached out and hugged Doreen as if she had always known her. "Oh, yes, certainly you're welcome. Come right in. Let me get some lemonade to freshen you up."

The warm voice and pleasant smile brought tears to Doreen's eyes.

They talked for a while, then Manerva asked,

"Would you come with us to our services tonight? We don't have a preacher, but Ben, my husband, and some of the others talk, then we pray together."

"I'd love to come," Doreen said. "Maybe I could preach for you if it would be all right with everyone."

"Oh, I was hoping you'd tell me you are a preacher. I could just tell from the way you were talking. I'm anxious to hear you preach. Don't worry about it, I know it will be all right with everybody. We need teaching so bad, God must have sent you here."

At church some friends pulled the Givens to one side and said, "We brought Doreen up from Tulsa where we've been visiting our family. She was at their house one day and asked us if we had any Pentecostal people where we live. We told her we knew one family. She said, 'Could I ride up there with you?' We asked, 'Do you know the Givens?' She said, 'No, but if they're Pentecostal I'll be welcome when I get there.' Hope it was all right with you. We told her she could come."

"Yes, yes! It sure was all right. I think God sent us just what we need," Manerva answered.

Revival began that night. The Givens drank in every word Doreen preached and decided to invite her to be a guest in their home. She taught them the Word every day and preached in the church every night. They wouldn't let her rest. The excitement of learning inflamed their hearts.

One day Manerva confessed, "The Caseys told us about the Holy Ghost, but I didn't see much need for it, and Ben didn't understand it either, so we never did anything about it."

Doreen began to concentrate on leading them to a recognition of their need of being baptized in the Holy Spirit.

Revival continued for over a month. Several friends from Winona, a town about eight or ten miles from Pershing, also attended the services. When Doreen closed the meeting they invited her to preach in Winona. They found an abandoned mechanic's garage (more precisely a *shed*, for both ends of the structure were open and its floor was dirt), built a pulpit, found some benches somewhere, and started revival meetings. Many souls were saved and gradually the congregation grew. They repaired the building and asked Doreen to stay as pastor after the meetings were over. They found her a place to live near the church.

The Givens decided to make Winona their home church, but Ben continued to teach a Bible study in Pershing.

In 1925 Matthew and Ruth Thompson came to the church for revival meetings. When the meeting ended Doreen asked them if they would consider taking the church to pastor because she felt it was time for her to go. They consented.

Ben continued to teach, dwelling more and more on the baptism in the Holy Spirit. Several were baptized under his guidance, but he and Manerva still had not been filled. In spite of that fact God persistently spoke to Ben's heart concerning full-time ministry. Ben resisted.

"Lord, I know You sent Doreen to teach me, and now the Thompsons, but I'm just not able to preach. I just can't do it," he would pray.

One day he said, "Nervy, for some reason I feel like we ought to go to Tulsa and visit my Grandma Givens. I'd like for her to see the girls. And I'd like for them to know some of their kin, even if I haven't known any of them."

They found Delilah Givens, a tiny lady of seventy-six, living with her sister. After their visit, as they prepared to leave, she said, "Wait a minute. I'm going home with you. While I get my things packed you put my feather bed in somewhere. I never go anywhere without it."

The only place Ben could find for the bed was on top of the car. They tied it down and returned home—Grandma, feather bed, and all. She stayed with them eight months. During that time she told Ben much about his father.

"He's awful sick, but he just keeps preaching. He's been everywhere, preaching on street corners, in old schoolhouses, in the mines, anywhere he gets a chance. He goes wherever he can pick up some work; mining or carpentry work is what he knows best. It's awful hard on him. He's not been well for many years.

"I've got a Bible of his I want to give you. He let me have it the last time I saw him."

She went to her trunk and brought out what appeared to be a black New Testament. She handed it to Ben, who looked at her with a quizzical expression, for all she had given him was the cover of a Bible—no pages, just the cover.

She said, "David was preaching on the streets in Wichita, Kansas, and a man snatched the Bible out of his hand, cursed him, and tore all the pages out, then threw it on the ground. Your father picked up the backs, glued them together, and that's what he carried on the streets to preach out of.

"The people didn't know he wasn't actually reading the Scriptures. He didn't need the inside. He had it so memorized he could have rewrote it anyway."

Ben learned that Charles F. Parham believed that Christians should live by faith and preachers should never take offerings in their meetings. If someone wanted to give something, take it, but don't ask for it. He believed that God would provide for all of their needs.

When Ben's father began preaching under Parham's Apostolic Faith Movement, he lived what he had been taught. He was forced to work to support his family while he spread the gospel, moving about from town to town. Many times he worked twelve or more hours, then ministered at night. Often he didn't sleep for twenty-four to thirty-six hours. He preached throughout Kansas, Missouri, Colorado, Arizona, Oklahoma, and many other states.

"Oh, God," Ben prayed, "I know you're calling me to continue my father's ministry. You're telling me he didn't finish what he wanted to do, and I must go complete his work. Even if Nervy would go with me, I can't drag her and the girls around like that, just doing without and suffering so much. I can't do it!"

Ben continued his Bible studies, and he and Manerva faithfully witnessed to their families. Manerva's parents, brothers and sisters and their spouses, along with her uncle Ed Slavens and his family, were soon all saved. Even Ben's mother and stepfather occasionally attended church with them, although they refused to become too closely associated with the Pentecostals.

As Ben agonized, his prayers bounced back to him and the Lord seemed far away. Satan tormented him with thoughts that Manerva wouldn't go. *She'll tell you if you want to preach just go ahead. But she won't let the girls go hungry or cold or without schooling just so you can run around all over the country. She'll kick you out of your home and tell you not to come back,* he seemed to say.

Ben prayed harder. The Lord reminded him that he had not done what he was asked to do.

Early one morning before Ben started home after his night shift job he knelt behind a large gasoline tank and surrendered his life to God's service.

"Father," he cried out, "I'll do what You want me to do even if it costs me my wife and children. I am willing to sacrifice the rest of my life to serve You. How could I do less? With Your help I promise to do my best to spread the truth You've shown me. When things get tough don't let me forget this prayer I'm praying to You now, and help me not to forget the vision You've given to me."

He walked home by the back trails so no one would hear his sobs.

Manerva was in the kitchen preparing breakfast. Ben put his arms around her and trembled as he spoke, "Nervy, I've got something to confess to you."

She hesitantly put her arms around him, and asked, "What is it, Ben?"

"Well, Sweetheart, God's been calling me to preach."

A smile flickered across Manerva's mouth. She said, "Honey, I've been knowing that for a long time. I'm willing to go anywhere you go and help you regardless of what happens. Me and the girls will pray for you and we'll go with you and suffer with you. We'll do anything. We plan to stick with you no matter what. Now you just let go and let God use you."

Ben raised his head and in quiet serenity said, "Thank You, Lord, for Your unfailing love."

He looked again at Manerva. "You'll never know how scared I was to tell you."

"Yes, I do know, and I know why," she said. "You always knew how your mother was against your dad's interest in Pentecostal people. The main reason you learned to hate him so much was because she was mad at him. She put that hate in you. All because he wanted to do right and she thought he'd disgraced all of you. You were afraid I'd do that to your children. Well, I won't. I'm proud of you, and our children are proud of you, too. Please, don't ever forget that, 'cause we need you as much as you need us."

Ben kissed her, then asked, "How in the world did you know that I'd been called to preach?"

"Just by the change I kept seeing in you. And the way you've got your head in the Bible day and night. When you're not working you're reading or telling me what you've read. You keep helping everybody get the Holy Ghost, even if you don't have it yourself. I never saw anything like it in all my life."

The devil and his lies were smothered by the Givens' love for each other and the call of God on their lives.

8

Holy Ghost Sermon

It was summertime, 1926. Ben worked the swing shift, checking out at midnight. One night as he walked home from work he noticed that the house was dark. *Funny,* he thought, *Nervy usually leaves the light on even if she goes to bed.*

"Manerva!" he called out as he opened the door. No one answered. "Guess she's still at church. Think I'll just go on to bed; she'll be here in a few minutes. She ought not to have gone without me. She could have waited till next week when my shift changes and I can go with her. It's just too dangerous if something goes wrong with that car."

Sleep wouldn't come. One o'clock, two o'clock, three o'clock—still no sign of his family.

"She's probably out having a high-heeled time while I'm here worrying myself to death. She should of brought the girls on home when church was over. They just don't need to be out traipsing around at this hour."

Just before four o'clock the car pulled into the drive. Ben turned over with his face to the wall and covered his head.

"Daddy, Daddy!" five-year-old Pauline called as she bounced into his room ahead of everyone else. "You can't guess what Mother has!"

"Well, she better have something good, coming in here this time of night," he grumbled.

"She has, she has! Daddy, Mother got the Holy Ghost tonight."

Manerva entered the bedroom, her face filled with joy. "Oh, Ben," she said, "I'm so sorry you weren't there when I received it. It's real! It's real! Honey, I'll always wish you'd been there."

Ben raised his head, looked at Manerva, and pouted, "I don't know why you got it first. I've tried and done everything possible to receive the Holy Ghost and haven't got it yet. I think God's just being partial to you." He turned his back to them again and pulled the covers up.

All week he pouted. But he saw such a change in Manerva's life, he could hardly wait until he could get to church. The first night, he went to the altar and began to wait and tarry, ask and pray for the Baptism.

While he was praying the Lord laid him out on the floor. His head and feet came up, and the Lord lifted his body about a foot off the floor. He hung in midair as if in a sling. Ben's mother was there and saw what happened. She ran to him, thinking he was dead, and touched him. The power of the Lord knocked her to the floor. Ben immediately dropped and regained consciousness.

He later told how the Lord had shown him his father and the letter he had received from Ben's hand so long ago. The words of hate on its pages stood out like black snakes crawling on white sand. He did not realize until that moment that he had never completely forgiven his father.

Ben cried uncontrollably. After several hours Manerva's uncle and aunt helped him home. He went into the bedroom and fell to the floor, still sobbing and begging forgiveness. Uncle Ed knelt beside him and prayed, "Lord, lay part of this heavy burden on me. Ben can't carry all of it alone." After the prayer Ben began to feel better.

The next night the Givens asked the Thompsons and the evangelist to come to their house the next day for supper. Ben worked until three o'clock. They would eat early and have time to get to church. Manerva had everything ready and on the table when Ben came home.

He said, "You folks just go ahead and eat, I'm not eating."

Ruth Thompson asked, "Why aren't you eating?"

"I'm going to fast until I get the Holy Ghost," he answered.

"All right," she said, "if you don't eat, then we don't eat. Manerva, just cover the table with a cloth, and let's all pray. The Lord can fill him with the Holy Ghost, and then we'll all eat."

About an hour later a warmth came into the room. Then it grew quiet. Then Ben began to speak in a heavenly language. He rose to his feet and danced. Manerva joined him and they rejoiced together in a beautiful dance unto the Lord.

In the spring of 1927 Ben entered the drugstore in Pawhuska.

"Ben," the druggist said, "I've been wanting to see you. There's a magazine here that lists names of people trying to locate relatives of people who's died. There's a David Givens listed. Is he any kin of yours?"

"Yes," Ben answered.

"Then take this. There's a daughter's name listed to write to. She's trying to find his family."

The article read: "On December 27, 1925, David Givens died in Phoenix, Arizona. Please contact his daughter, Pauline Derr, in Phoenix, if you know the whereabouts of his children by a former marriage."

Before Ben reached his home he stopped the car and walked into the woods. Special shades of tender green were bringing new hope to the winter dead hills. Bright red leaves flamed on bushes here and there. Sounds of a small stream just awakening underneath a blanket of ice competed with the call of birds for attention.

Ben picked up a rock and aimed it at another one resting on the bottom of the stream. The waves quickly widened and spread from the splash, ending at the banks, pushing tender foliage to and fro. He sat down on a fallen, rotting tree sprouting new growth from its roots; he felt a deep sense of calm and peace. Instead of the bitterness and anger Ben had known all his life at the mention of his father's name, he felt the healing that brings forth new life. He knelt on the ground and vowed to carry on his father's mission, giving and forgiving like the man he had never known. Ben felt he could do that much—even if now his father never would hear from him about his change of heart.

For the next year the Givens were faithful to the Winona church, working, visiting, witnessing, and learning from their pastors. Ruth Thompson did most of the preaching and teaching while Matthew, the quiet worker, faithfully served behind the scenes.

During the Thompsons' pastorate the congregation built a new church building and affiliated with the new Assemblies of God organization.

The night the church body voted to join the Assemblies of God the Givens and one other couple voted no. They were uneasy about taking such a step and feared dissension within the body. After seeing the results of the vote, they apologized. Ben became the first charter member on their church roster, Manerva was second, with the other couple, third and fourth. The church continued to grow both spiritually and numerically.

The people in Winona had a mind to work, a mind to give, and a mind to love. They worked together as one person in their little church. They enjoyed giving. The oil field workers were paid good money, so in addition to paying their tithes they would take groceries and staple goods to the pastors' home. Ruth had a cabinet where she stored the food they couldn't use. When the cabinet was full she would tell her husband that they were going to hear of someone in need because they were getting too much. Sure enough they would hear of someone, so they would empty the shelves and start all over again.

Ruth Thompson became the Givens' spiritual mother (they would never lose contact with her). The Thompsons moved to Florida after their Winona pastorate and remained there pastoring or doing evangelistic work until Matthew's death.

Later Ruth married Reverend Garrett, retired superintendent of the Northern Florida District of the Assemblies of God. They pastored the Durant Assembly of God until his death. Ruth continued pastoring for a while and now lives near the church, officially retired, yet continually on call to pray or minister anywhere she is needed. Many hundreds join the Givens in calling her their spiritual mother.

In 1928, Ben was still teaching Bible studies in Pershing but had not yet preached a sermon.

"I think the Lord is leading me to make some kind of change. What do you think?" he asked Manerva.

"I feel the same way," she replied. "You don't seem to want to start preaching here, and I think God just might be calling you to some other place."

"I've considered moving to Missouri. Back up to Lebanon. Since your folks have all gone back there, we could keep teaching them and maybe lead some of the others to the Lord. I'm still afraid to try to preach to anybody but home folks."

"If that's what you want to do, that's what we'll do. But I don't know why you're so afraid to preach. Your Bible studies show how deep you are in knowledge of the Word. I wouldn't be afraid for you to preach anywhere."

Ben resigned his job, and Manerva began to pack. She looked at her home, so beautiful, so perfect with its clean walls, starched curtains, spotless floors, and polished furniture.

"Oh, Lord," she prayed, "I've loved living here. It's where we found You. It was our first real home. I'll miss the comfort it's given us. I'll miss my friends here and in Winona. Oh, I'll miss the church so much, and the Thompsons. You know how I love them.

"But I'll sing a song of praise to You forever because You've called us to serve You in the ministry. I'll go wherever You lead us, I'll suffer whatever I need to, to serve You. I'll obey Your voice, Your call, and I will always reverence and hold that call as something special from You."

Shortly after, the Givens moved. Ben went to work operating the cofferdam pumps in the powerhouse of the Tunnel Dam being built on the Niangua River, a part of the Lake of the Ozarks project. A bus provided transportation to and from work. He worked the graveyard shift, which freed him to have home prayer meetings and Bible studies in the early evenings.

At first only relatives attended. Later they began to bring friends, and Ben had to find larger places to meet, such as abandoned schoolhouses, larger homes, anything available. They met every night, but Sundays were all-day meetings. The people sang, testified, read the Bible to each other, and prayed, many times for hours. Still, Ben had not preached his first sermon.

One day Manerva's uncle Ed Slavens asked Ben, "You know that community church up in Eldridge?"

"Yes, what about it?"

"They let any organization come in there for two weeks at a time and hold meetings. A Pentecostal preacher from Springfield was there not long ago, but someone called him a false teacher, so he left. Now that feller that chased him off has challenged anyone to debate this baptism in the Holy Ghost with him. I just thought you might like to give it a try."

"I'll pray about it," Ben replied.

After many hours of prayer and fasting Ben decided to accept the challenge.

"Uncle Ed, if you'll take care of everything for me, I'll do it." Ben's voice trembled with fear as he spoke.

"All right, I'll set up the meeting and tell everybody. You just get ready."

Ben began to study 1 Corinthians 14:18 and made his first sermon notes on an ink blotter from an empty writing tablet. On the day of the meeting his body shook so hard he couldn't pray. But unknown to him Manerva and her mother fasted and prayed all day.

The challenger insisted that Ben be first. The church was full, and people were milling around outside. Ben pulled his trembling body up from the seat. His shoes felt heavy and too large as he moved toward the pulpit. His hands grasped the sides of the stand.

He said, "This is the first time in my life to stand as a preacher in a preacher's place. Let's all bow our heads for prayer." He prayed a scared, rambling prayer, and said amen.

At that moment Ben felt God's anointing and ceased to see the people seated in front of him. He was aware of only one thing: spiritual waves like waves on an ocean. Scriptures came like gifts from the waves. He saw hands lifted. He saw tears. He heard praise. He felt he was walking on air, and strength poured into and all over him.

He watched the challenger rise from his seat and walk out. Ben never saw the man again.

The full gospel message, presented simply, broke down walls of inner darkness and freed emotions, not to hysterical and irrational actions, but to spiritual understandings never known before. People were so transformed by God they were amazed at the changes taking place in their hearts. They moved with haste to set right the sins that loomed before them. A bootlegger on that day poured out a barrel of whiskey; later he became the pastor of that community church, affiliated it with the Assemblies of God movement, and remained its pastor until his death.

9

A Brush Arbor Work

The next spring, in Ira, Missouri, Ben built his first brush arbor. After the rainstorm on the first night, when the song leader and his friends planned to burn down the brush arbor, glorious revival came. Nothing stopped it.

Often services lasted until time for Ben to go to work. The next day, in order to study without going to sleep, he stood at the kitchen table with a tall box for his Bible to rest on. He stayed there until God anointed him. Then he preached the sermon in his mind and prayed silently, too weary to speak aloud. There was a zeal, an earnestness, a freshness about every sermon. Ben completely devoted himself to his call. Manerva stood by him, fasting and praying long hours every day. This contagious dedication and excitement changed lives forever.

All summer joyful singing floated from the arbor, passing the hills, touching the treetops, and dancing toward the silent sky. Was Isaiah transported through time to view such a scene when he wrote, "The mountains and the hills shall break forth before you into singing, and all the trees of the field shall clap their hands"?

The singing reflected inner longings being fulfilled. People hungered not for natural food but for spiritual truths and needed to worship with freedom and honesty.

Yet, on a still and quiet autumn evening after the singers hushed, Ben stood behind his cigar-box pulpit and told the people he was going to close the brush arbor meeting. In the chill of the pale dusk the congregation silently leaned forward and drew close together.

Ben longed to stay with them. He wanted to be their pastor and build a church but felt inadequate and unprepared for such a task.

Finally a young man said quietly, "We won't have no preacher. We won't have no one to help us."

Ben looked at the man who had spoken. He sat near the front of the arbor with his family and had attended all the meetings. He was young but the depleted heritage of the land had sweated the youth from his face. His worn overalls and blue chambray shirt reflected the work of a rub board, homemade soap, and spring water. The tops of his dusty, plowing shoes, with barnyard mud clinging around the edge of the heels, still had some brown in them.

Ben remembered a time during the summer when the young man had come to him wanting to trade thirty acres of land with a two-room cabin and a spring that never went dry, for Ben's cow and calf, plus six dollars.

Ben had looked at the place and asked, "Could I look at the head of the spring?"

The man hesitated, "Oh, it's up there about three hundred yards. You don't want to walk that far, do you?"

"I don't mind the walk. I'd like to see it," Ben said.

"Well, Preacher, I'll take you up there, but you better not see nothing except the spring."

Moonshine whiskey stills were often found nestled among the blackjack trees during those Prohibition days. And sure enough, just as Ben thought, there was one cooking away.

"It belongs to me and my neighbor," the man said. "That's how I get a living for my family. There ain't no work here in these hills, you know."

Ben and the man sat down beneath a huge tree, its bowing branches shadowing the spring. Ben explained to his friend how alcohol had wrecked his life before he had found Christ. "I couldn't give it up before then, but with Christ filling my life, I had no room for anything else. It was the easiest thing I ever did."

"I guess maybe you're right. I guess that's what I'll have to do."

Soon after that he came to the altar with his wife, and they made their confession to God.

Now, months later, Ben looked at the man and his family in the arbor and wondered how God would provide spiritual leadership for them.

Ben looked near the center of the arbor at another family, holding their baby girl. He remembered not long before how the tiny infant had become ill, and he and Manerva had been called to pray for her. It was raining and they feared they couldn't make it over the rain-soaked, rutty road far in the hills where the family lived. But they decided to try anyway.

"We don't have money for gas," Manerva said.

"We'll borrow it till payday," Ben replied.

They threw in an axe and shovel and left early, long before daylight.

"If we can stay out of the wagon ruts maybe we won't get stuck," Ben said, guiding and turning the slipping, sliding car.

No sooner had he spoken than the car slipped into a deep rut, ripping a tire and sinking far into the mud.

Ben cut poles to pry the wheel up, changed the tire, then threw rocks and brush under the wheels. Manerva drove the car out while Ben pushed and pulled, keeping the wheels out of the ruts. The heavy rain soaked him and the wheels threw mud all over him. Manerva threw an old blanket around him, and they went on. Several times they repeated the ordeal before they reached the house.

The family was poverty-stricken. Ben and Manerva had never seen such deprivation. The children cried from hunger, cold, and sickness. The baby's swollen head gave evidence of her near death. Ben and Manerva walked back outside and stood under the leaking porch and began to cry. Ben stepped down and looked up into the heavens and rain fell in his face. He prayed, "God, make us worthy just this one time to pray for a dying baby and an unfortunate home."

They went back into the room and laid their hands on the frail body and prayed again. Suddenly the swelling began to go down.

Happy and rejoicing, the Givens climbed into the car and started back home. "A hot cup of coffee would sure be good right now, wouldn't it, Nervy?" Ben asked, then placed a gentle arm around her wet shoulders and held her tight.

Thanking God they traveled home over the same road without any trouble. Ben went to his job tired but his soul burst with joy as he told his working buddies what God had done. Some of the men were related to the family, and many accepted God when the news spread around the community.

Now this family listened to Ben tell them he must close the brush arbor meeting. They, too, would need spiritual leadership.

"Guess we can't ask you to stay," someone said.

A soft breeze moved in, flickering the gas torchlight and ruffling the dried brush roof.

"Others got to get saved, too," someone else said.

Getting saved was different from anything these people had ever done. They experienced an inner awakening and felt a closeness to God, a sense of belonging not known before.

Being baptized in the Holy Spirit reinforced their newfound existence. They read the Scriptures day and night, poring over passages alone and together, being enlightened one by one. Never had they felt so untroubled in their souls.

The Givens had watched as the direction of these country people's lives had changed. God was in everything. They prayed before making the simplest decision. The women bought material and made clothing for their families instead of buying lipstick, rouge, and face powder. They bought a pair of stockings for the price of fingernail polish. They carefully considered such things as shoes for each child.

No more Saturday afternoon movies or evening dancing and drinking parties. That time was spent shampooing hair, taking baths, polishing shoes, last minute checks on everyone's clothes, making sure all the mending and pressing were done for Sunday services, doing the evening chores, and then going to the arbor for another worship service.

The men threw away cigarettes, crushed whiskey stills, burned gambling cards, and began to take control of their lives. They rejoiced and praised God as they plowed their fields. They thanked Him for food and shelter as they fed and cared for their meager stock.

The people didn't always understand the reasons for the changes in their lives, except it seemed pleasing to God. They loved the Lord and were ever mindful of His Spirit teaching them to be holy and clean in everything they did.

The arbor became the center of their social activities. They came every night for services and arrived at nine o'clock Sunday morning. Often they brought their lunches and stayed all day. They worshiped until noon, or later, then shared good food, good humor, great blessings, and unforgettable fellowship, binding them together in bonds of love never known to them before.

The men and boys usually rushed home in the early evening to do the chores. Then they hurried back to the arbor to worship God and testify of His blessings and answered prayers, sometimes remaining there until well after midnight. Many walked home tired in body but refreshed in soul and spirit, ready for another week of toil that usually began at four-thirty in the morning.

But Ben feared that when he closed the brush arbor, the people would scatter and be destroyed spiritually. As Ben looked upon the people that night, like Jesus seeing the multitudes, he saw a pasture of sheep, mangled and torn, left dead and dying from mortal wounds—sheep without a shepherd. Ben raised his hands toward heaven and cried out to God to send a shepherd into the field. He longed to stay. Perhaps someday he could return. But the thrusting he felt tonight was a prompting from the Lord to move on.

Then an extraordinary thing happened.

"Preacher," said the young man who had owned the whiskey still. "Don't you worry none about us. We'll do fine. Maybe we can meet in the schoolhouse this winter and some of us can do some of the preaching. God's been talking a little bit to me. It's hard to think about it, but I guess I'll have to if God says to."

"We aim to have a church around here somewhere," the song leader said. "It may not be right here, but it's going to be somewhere so we can worship like we want to. Nobody's got any money, but we're going to do something. I'll help out with some of that preaching, too. God's been leading me that way lately."

Before Ben could speak another voice came from the audience. "He's been calling me, too."

Ben raised his voice to heaven in praise and thanksgiving. The people would stay together. In his first brush arbor revival over fifty people had been saved and filled with the Holy Spirit, and three had been called into the ministry.

"Where are you going to be preaching? Are you leaving here altogether?" they wanted to know.

"No, we're going to stay in Lebanon for a while, where we've been living, and work from there, like we've done here."

"Then I aim to see that the people come over and help you out. I've got an old beat-up cattle truck and some others have one, and we'll just fill them up and come over."

"We're sure going to be looking for you, and we're sure much obliged to you," Ben said. "You know this is Manerva's birthplace, and her folks are back here now. We'll be back from time to time, and we'll help you out when we can."

Before the service ended, Pauline, who had recently turned nine, and Maxine, almost seven, were asked to sing. Glowing with expectation, they bounced to the front. Manerva strummed a few notes on a borrowed guitar, and the girls began to sing about Jesus going a little further than His followers—all the way to Calvary.

That night, long after Ben had fallen asleep, Manerva heard muffled sobs coming from the girls' bedroom. She slipped in and found Pauline with her face buried in her pillow, crying. Taking her in her arms, she asked, "What is it, Honey? What's the matter?"

"I hate to think about leaving Lebanon school. We just got started. I don't want to leave my friends."

"Sweetheart, we're not going to leave for a while. Maybe not for a long time. Daddy wants to preach around here as much as he can so you don't have to change schools."

"But we will have to go. I will have to leave sometime. Mother, I liked it at Pershing, and we had to leave there. I remember my friends, and I won't ever see them again. It's not so hard for Maxine; she didn't go there very long and she probably can't even remember the schoolhouse, or her friends, or even Oklahoma."

"Yes, I can, too," Maxine said as she turned over and raised up.

"Girls," Manerva said, "I thought your name was Givens."

"It is!" they both said.

"It must not be, 'cause Givens are tough. They take things they have to and don't complain. Things get rough in this life sometimes, and we all have to do things we don't want to do. But God knew the Ben Givens family could move where He needed them and suffer whatever they had to, in order to tell people about Jesus dying for them."

"Did He know I'd have to leave my friends?" Pauline asked.

"Yes, He did. But He was sure His two little warriors could do it, just for Him."

"I'm not going to cry when we leave," Maxine said. Then she yawned and closed her eyes.

Pauline threw her arms around her mother's neck and whispered in her ear, "Mother, I'm a Givens. I won't cry anymore."

Manerva lay beside Ben listening to his even, restful sleep until the early hours of the morning.

Maxine Givens, 5; Pauline Givens, 7

10
Pressing On

The years passed quickly after Ben closed the brush arbor revival in Ira. The people of Ira remained true to their word and came by truckloads to help wherever Ben preached. Sometimes meetings lasted until midnight or later. Then they would pray until daybreak. The people helped the Givens with great sincerity and sacrifice. A deep bond of Christian fellowship and service united them in one of the most joyful experiences of their lives—helping other people get saved.

When work at the Tunnel Dam ended Ben went to Linn Creek and found a job clearing timber, piling it in great heaps to burn, preparing a bed for the Lake of the Ozarks to flow into after the dam was completed. Because his new job provided no bus service and Ben did not own a car, he camped near the site with other workers and some of their families. Ben worked all day and then held services by the light of the burning logs. Several were saved and baptized in the Holy Spirit.

After the Linn Creek job was over, it was difficult for Ben to find work. The nation was in a severe depression. During these difficult times the Givens were forced to concentrate on survival. Many times they would cut wood from free government land and haul it to a wagon yard in town to sell for seventy-five cents a load. Sometimes, if it didn't sell, they left it overnight, and often it was stolen.

The Givens' ministry had always been a gift of love to their Saviour. They had never taken an offering. They felt humble and grateful when someone helped them. Their first grocery shower came from a man who claimed to be an infidel, but could quote as many Scriptures as Ben. He enjoyed arguing with anyone.

One day he asked Ben to preach on the third heaven mentioned in 2 Corinthians 12:2. Ben preached, explaining it the best he could. The man came to Ben after the service, patted him on the back, and said, "Son, you're doing very well for a young upstart."

"Thank you," Ben replied.

"Do you have any syrup buckets or paper sacks around?" the man asked.

"I think we can find some."

"Come over to my house sometime soon and bring them."

Ben and Manerva found several and took them over the next day. The man and his wife filled the buckets with lard, black-eyed peas, beans, and other things. They filled the sacks with potatoes, a ham, a slab of bacon, and much more.

The man never knew that the Givens were completely out of food. But God always met their need without anyone knowing it. Ben and Manerva thanked the man and praised God for His blessings.

Later, Ben noticed that the man didn't argue on the Scriptures as he usually did, but seemed quiet and thoughtful. In a short time he accepted the Lord and soon after, died of a heart attack.

The Givens held so many revival meetings in those

small communities in the very heart of America they could never remember all the events or where they took place. But, once, when Ben was preaching, a gang of men rode up on horseback. One dismounted and stalked down the aisle with a rope, looped and ready, to put around Ben's neck to drag him behind his horse until Ben agreed to leave. The people rose to defend Ben and the gospel he preached. A fight started.

An unsaved man who had worked with Ben on the Lake of the Ozarks happened to be in the service. He dragged eight of the men off their horses and knocked them out. The rest of the men fled.

Another time, Ben preached about Paul's conversion on the road to Damascus. A mean man who had many knife fights was in the service. The next day as the man walked along the side of a hill he said, "God, that preacher lied. You never knocked anyone down. If You did, why don't You just knock me down?"

Down he went! He hit the sharp flint rocks, cutting his hands. He started to get up, but he was pitched forward, cutting his face and nose. He struggled and almost got to his feet but fell forward again, skinning his knees and shins.

That night the man went to church and publicly asked Ben's forgiveness for thinking he had lied. He showed the people his knees, shins, and hands. Ben didn't have to make an altar call—people came running down the aisle to find God as their Saviour.

Only once during this time were Ben and Manerva's spirits low. A church asked Ben to preach each Sunday for two months during a cold winter. Their circuit rider had become ill and the church needed a preacher.

The Givens packed a lunch every Sunday, filled a

lantern with oil to keep the girls warm, and stayed in the church building all day. Ben preached morning and evening. No one ever asked them to their home. They received only thirty-five cents for the entire two months. They felt discouraged and rejected. But from this experience God taught them to walk by faith, to preach faith and love, and to be happy in every place and circumstance He led them.

Another time Ben got permission to use a small country schoolhouse for a meeting. But before the first service could be held, three men drove out to his home to see him. Ben heard the truck slow down, so he went to the door and watched it stop. The wooden slats of the cattle bed clapped together in nervous rhythm while dust from the unpaved road rolled on, heedless of the stop. The men got out, left the doors open, and started toward the house. Ben pushed open the screen door and walked out on the porch.

"Howdy," he said.

"You Ben Givens?"

"Yes, what can I do for you?"

"We're trustees from the school."

"Won't you come in?"

"No, we'll just stand out here. Don't have much time. Got some cattle hauling to do later. Sure been good weather this spring, ain't it?"

"Yes, sir, it sure has," Ben answered as he stepped off the porch.

One of the men cleared his throat, then said, "Mr. Givens, what we come to ask you is, what did you start from?"

"What do you mean?" Ben asked.

"What we mean is, who do you work for?"

"I work for the Lord. He's in full control of my life."

"We know that. But what organization do you belong to?"

Ben was beginning to understand. "I don't belong to any organization."

"Listen," they said firmly, "rumor has it that you're a holy roller, and we don't want any of them in here, so don't come back to the schoolhouse. You're not going to get in."

"But I got permission from one of the other trustees. I forget his name, but I can take you to him."

"That won't be necessary. We've already talked to him, and he goes along with us now. He didn't know you was holy rollers."

"What difference does that make?" Ben asked.

"Any other denomination could of come in, but we don't want you people getting started around here. Somebody's got to take a stand."

There was no need to argue. Ben thought for a moment, then asked, "How about the school land? Is it all right if we build a brush arbor on that?"

The men looked at each other, knowing there could be legal problems if they refused.

"As far as I can see, it would be all right to build a brush arbor," one man said. He spit on the ground, then turned back to the others, "What do you all think?"

The others finally nodded. "Go ahead, but don't cut any big trees, and be sure and clean up the mess when you leave."

After the men drove away Ben went in the house. Manerva was waiting by the door.

"Just what we was afraid of, Nervy—they won't let us use the schoolhouse."

"I know, I figured it out. Honey, we can't let a little

thing like that get us down. God sent us here, and He'll help us find a way to preach."

"They said we could build a brush arbor."

"Then what are we waiting for?"

"I hate to put you through all that. It would have been easier if they'd left things alone. Besides, what difference does it make if we're inside or outside, we're still holy rollers. Just wanting to show their authority, is all I can figure out."

"Hush up, Ben Givens. I've never been afraid of work in my whole life, and I'm not afraid of it now. You just get us a crosscut saw and an axe. Me and the girls will help you, and we'll have a place built before you know it. We can start our meeting next Sunday. Word will get around. Might even be better. More will know about it when they see the arbor going up."

Many times the Givens grew weary and tired. Yet amidst the weariness the burden was light in the excitement of the gospel. Jesus was their Shield and Companion. He taught them by His Spirit not to fear but to press on. They felt excited and uplifted in His presence and lived with a singleness of mind: to obey the Lord and preach His message. Every morning they prayed together, "Dear Lord, this is Your new day. Help us to exalt You somehow this day."

11

A Hard Call

In November 1931 Ben received a letter from his brother. He opened it and began to read.

"Manerva!" Ben called. "Abe wants us to come down to South West City and hold a meeting. Says we can get an old storefront and rent some folding chairs from over in Joplin. We can stay with him and his family and send the girls to school there."

"Well, what do you think?" Manerva asked.

"Guess it would encourage Abe. He hasn't been a Christian very long. He made fun of us in the beginning, but now he's really trying. It's a long way from home—about two hundred miles, I think. We'd be out of our territory. I don't know if I'm ready to get that far away."

Manerva put her hands on her hips, turned her head to one side, looked at Ben through the corner of her eyes, and said, "You've preached around here for two years. Don't you think it's about time you spread out a little?"

"Maybe. I just hope I'm ready. Let's fast and pray about it, then decide. Abe says it won't be easy. People are still hard against Pentecost down there."

"Are you saying that your girls are softies?" Manerva teased.

"No, I know better than that."

"Daddy, we can do it," said Maxine.

Pauline joined in, "We don't mind. We got to stay here in Lebanon longer than we thought. It might even be fun going to school in South West City."

"You're the beatin'est family I ever had," Ben laughed.

"We're the only family you'll ever have," Maxine said, climbing into his lap for a big hug.

Even though the Givens had been members of the Assemblies of God church in Pershing, they still did not understand how to become associated with the organization as ministers. They had not met anyone to guide them and did not realize the strength and material help they could receive from an organization. They worked alone and suffered their persecutions with only relatives and friends to share their burdens.

In the little town of South West City, tucked in the corner of Missouri next to the borders of Oklahoma and Arkansas, the Givens would experience some of their most rewarding blessings. However, there they would also labor under their most severe opposition and for the first time disobey God's call on their lives.

They went to South West City with Manerva's sister and brother-in-law Ted and Joan Gentry and soon rented a few chairs and a piano. They brought some songbooks with them.

During the first service Ben noticed a young woman holding a small baby sitting apart from everyone. He thought she was very considerate to keep the baby from disturbing the others. He announced that his message was on adultery. All eyes turned toward the young mother. She started to cry.

Ben began. "Is adultery the unpardonable sin? No,

a thousand times no, and ten thousand times no, it isn't adultery."

He explained the unpardonable sin. Then he stated that all mistakes are covered with the blood of Jesus as soon as a sinner repents. God forgives and forgets everything.

The young woman came to the altar and confessed her sins to God. She then told Ben and Manerva that her baby was born out of wedlock, and she had become an outcast in the town. Pastors of two different churches had told her never to come back because of her sin. No one talked to or befriended her.

Ben taught the people until long into the night to love and to forgive her. He told them she was now clean and pure in God's sight and forgiven just like they were. The people asked forgiveness and accepted her as one of them.

Revival began, but so did persecution. People arrived from everywhere, and in the midst of souls being saved, others were telling the Givens to leave; they would not tolerate a holy roller meeting.

One night Ben stated from the pulpit that he had been a soldier in the United States Army. He had fought for freedom and that included freedom of religion. In desperation he put an American flag on the ceiling above his pulpit. The abuse continued. Ben called the sheriff, but there was only one. Somehow he managed to referee a basketball game in a neighboring town every night.

The angry people tried all kinds of physical and verbal abuse to make them leave. They spit in Ben's face, drew knives on him, put pistols in his ribs, and threatened his family with bodily harm. One night some people disturbed the services by burning gunpowder on the stove, claiming it was an old Indian sign of war.

But in spite of the difficulties souls continued to be saved and filled with the Holy Spirit. One cold night a farmer and his wife brought two neighbor ladies. After the service their car wouldn't start. The Givens took them home. When he stopped to let the first woman out, her husband cursed Ben and the farmer. He took his wife's Bible and tore it to pieces. Then he threatened to kill Ben if he ever saw him with his wife again.

A few nights later this man's stepdaughter received the Holy Spirit. She didn't have a ride home. The Givens gave her their bed and sat by the fireplace all night. Pauline and Maxine sat with them. The man came the next day and threatened Ben with a pistol to leave. Ben told him he would obey the Lord, not man, and would not go until God told him to.

Manerva and her sister Joan led the song services, played the piano, and worked at the altars. One night laryngitis hit Ben. Going home from church he whispered to Manerva that she would have to preach the next night.

"Oh, no!" she cried, "God called you to preach—not me!"

"God's been calling you, too."

"How did you know that?" she quickly asked.

He laughed. "Because almost every night when you get up to testify, you preach half my sermon before I get to preach it."

"Well, I don't care! I can't do it!"

Early the next morning Ben woke Manerva and whispered, "I still can't talk so you'll have to get a message ready for tonight." He told her that he was going with the men to cut wood for the church stove and would be back around noon.

She began to pray and cry, “Oh, God, I can’t get up before those people. I wouldn’t know what to say.”

When Ben returned he whispered, “Where’s Nervy?”

“She’s still in her bedroom, hasn’t been out all morning. Sometimes we hear her praying, sometimes crying.”

Ben opened the door and found her on the floor. He knelt and took her in his arms. “Sweetheart,” he whispered, “haven’t you got a message yet?”

“I stayed in here and fasted and prayed for you to receive your healing so you can preach. I’ve been praying for you,” she sobbed.

“Hasn’t God given you anything to preach about?”

“Yes, He really did. But I can’t find it in the Bible. I’ve looked through it, and I can’t find it. It may not be a Scripture. I may have just thought it up.”

“What’s the Scripture?” Ben asked.

Manerva told him, and he immediately turned to the first Psalm. “Here it is.”

She looked at it, and the letters seemed to stand out from the Bible. She said, “If God gave me a message that I didn’t know was in the Bible, then God will be with me to preach that message. All right, Honey, I’ll try to preach for you.”

Joan led the songs that night and Abe did the preliminaries. He announced that his sister-in-law was going to preach her first sermon.

Well, I hope I am, thought Manerva. After she read the Scripture text the Holy Spirit seemed to take over. She felt as though she stood to one side and the Holy Spirit did all the work.

After the service two men came to the front.

"Lady," one spoke, "did I understand that this was your first sermon?"

"Yes, it was."

"You did so well, that's hard for us to believe. We are both ministers, he's Methodist, I'm Baptist."

I'm glad you didn't tell me that before the service, she thought to herself.

From that night on, for over fifty years, Manerva preached every other sermon in all their ministry together.

Shortly afterwards Ben announced he would be closing the meetings and if anyone would like to be baptized before he left they would have a baptismal service at the river, under the railroad bridge. The man who had threatened to kill Ben told him, "You baptize my stepdaughter and I'll drown the both of you. The undertaker'll fish you both out of the water."

Ben had fifteen candidates for baptism that day, but after they had all been baptized, he asked if there was anyone else. A girl bolted from the group and into the water. Ben immediately recognized her as the one he had been warned not to baptize. And her stepfather was among the onlookers. Ben took her through baptism. Her stepfather simply backed away.

The little congregation begged Ben to stay and become their pastor.

He refused.

"Are you sure it's God's will for us to go?" Manerva asked.

"I can't stay here. I'm not ready to pastor, and besides, its just too hard to make it. Look at how we've been treated, everybody fighting us, nobody giving us any money to live on. We need to settle down around Lebanon and put the girls back in school there. I think we'll get a farm somewhere and make a garden and crop. At least we won't starve."

"The people said they'd rent us a place, give us food and everything we needed, if we'd just start a church," Manerva reminded him.

"I know what they said, but I'm tired and we've been hit too hard. We're going home."

They rented a farm near Lebanon, and during Christmas vacation went to Decatur, Illinois, to visit Manerva's uncle. When they returned they found a notice tacked on the door stating that the place had been sold. They had thirty days to vacate the premises. They moved to another place with ten acres. Ben planned to work whenever he could, farm the land, and preach in the area.

God began to speak to Ben in a dream. Every night for five nights he dreamed that his house was burning with Manerva and the girls inside. He cried out, "Oh, God, it can't be! What have I left?"

A big hand appeared with Ben's Bible in it, showing its cardboard back that looked like dried beaten leather and the once white Johnson's Adhesive Tape holding the spine together. The cover's protective edge had crumbled like old lace curtains washed on a rub board.

Each time he had the dream Ben jumped out of the bed and, with Manerva, knelt and prayed.

One day the Givens returned from town. When they stopped the car, the dream came as a vision in daylight. God seemed to say, "I have called and have need of you. Will you heed My call?" Ben and Manerva fell on their knees and asked forgiveness for their neglect.

"We should have stayed in South West City," Ben confessed. "I felt it then, but I thought it would be too hard. I just didn't know what would happen to us."

"Then let's get back into God's work," Manerva said.

They committed all to God and said, "Yes, Lord, we'll heed Your call."

The Givens once again began to hold meetings in and around Ira.

One Sunday they started a meeting in the Markel School District. Ben read his text, looked out at the congregation, and spotted a Methodist preacher. Ben lost his train of thought. He began to stammer, and fell silent. Finally he began to cry.

A woman came to the altar to be saved, and Manerva prayed with her. The minister, a black man, came to Ben and asked, "My presence bothered you, didn't it?"

"Yes," Ben nodded.

The white-haired minister put his arm around the frightened young minister. They talked for hours. The old man assured Ben that if God was with him, the devil couldn't touch him. He concluded by saying, "If a man of God is sitting before you, his prayers and presence are all in your favor. And if anyone ever bothers you, just imagine they are cabbage heads out there, then let God have your tongue and mind."

In March 1932 the Givens family went to St. Louis for meetings. They began on Sunday night. Monday Maxine became desperately ill with pneumonia. On Tuesday the doctor put her in the hospital. Wednesday morning Manerva also fell ill with pneumonia and entered the same hospital. Ben closed the services on Thursday night. Three days later Manerva was moved to the death ward, but Maxine seemed better.

"Daddy, how's Mother?"

"She's awful sick and in lots of pain."

"Let's pray for her," Maxine decided.

After they prayed she said, "Daddy, you leave me and go visit Mother."

"They won't let me in the ward, and I need to stay with you."

"No," she protested. "Go see about Mother, then tell me how she is. I'll be all right till you get back." For nine years old, she was a little lady.

Ben watched up and down the hall until it was clear, then slipped into Manerva's room.

"Honey," she said as soon as she saw him, "something just happened to me. It was like a hot blanket fell all around me, and my pain left. I feel like I can go home."

Shortly after that she was moved out of the death ward, but Maxine grew worse. Ben wrestled with God day and night. He questioned God. The world lost its beauty.

Manerva was released from the hospital, but on March 26 she and Ben knelt by their baby's bed and with arms around her frail form felt Maxine gasp one final breath.

Four days later, Ben, Manerva, and Pauline sat on the front row in the little schoolhouse in Ira, Missouri, where they had held their first revival and built their first brush arbor. Ben and Manerva stared at a small pale-blue casket and did not understand. It held the still, quiet body of their younger daughter. They knew in a few moments the lid would be closed forever.

Manerva leaned closer to Pauline and held her tight. *Dear Lord,* she silently prayed, *thank You because we still have one little girl, but what do we do now? One is gone from us and we'll never see her on this earth again. Are You saying we ought to quit? Is that the reason You didn't heal her like You did the night we got saved?*

The deep lonely feeling Ben knew as a young boy crept back, and his soft, gentle heart felt as though it were dying, not because he had never had someone, but now because he had lost someone.

The Givens remembered that the family had willingly faced every hardship until now. All four had been blessed with a pioneer spirit, a carefree outlook, a determined disposition, and a knowledge that they were pleasing God. He had always brought them through with great joy.

A few days later Ben heard that the school building in Pershing, where Maxine had started school, had been torn down. He bought a portion of the Carthage granite cornerstone and had a tombstone made from it to mark Maxine's grave.

One day Ben said, "Sweetheart, maybe we ought to go back to St. Louis and finish our meetings. What do you think?"

"I've thought about that, too. I've also been thinking about all the years we've served God and all that's happened. My mind's had time to begin to sort out the good and forget the bad."

"Me, too. On the day of the funeral I started remembering the bad, but the good kept coming to me. I also looked at everybody around me and saw how God has changed their lives."

"Yes," Manerva said. "Our brothers and sisters are all coming around. Most of them are saved now. Even your mother keeps coming more and more to church. Some of the people at the funeral used to be so hard against us. But now, just think, they're serving God, and churches are being built for the first time around here."

"Most of them are getting the Holy Ghost, too," Ben said. "Your mother told me that while Maxine's body lay here she sat down by it for a minute, and a warm, comforting, heavenly love folded around her. She said she spoke some strange words and thinks it was the Spirit you and me have."

"It's all been worthwhile, hasn't it?" Manerva asked.

"Yes, and it makes me really sorry about questioning God. He knows why He took our little girl, and we've got to have faith and just rest in Him. He told us to come to Him when we're burdened and heavy laden and He will give us rest."

"I hope He'll forgive us and bless us again like He's done before," Manerva said.

"He will, Sweetheart. We'll just have to confess what we did wrong and pick up from there. I wish I could let things alone and not fail so much. You know, I can't count how many times I've been saved since I got saved."

12

The Preacher on Tenth Street

When the Givens returned to St. Louis, Ben got a job as a hod carrier on a construction site, for forty cents an hour, twelve hours a day. He preached every other night.

"Nervy, I've made a decision," he declared one evening before they left for church. "I've never taken an offering, but I'm going to start tonight."

"What's got into you?" Manerva asked. "We're doing all right."

"We're not doing all right, but that's not the point. The offering won't be for us. It's to help feed the hungry people I see all around this place. They're starving to death—little kids, men, women—everybody, just wandering around on the streets looking for food. I can't preach worrying about it, and they can't listen if they're hungry. I'm just not going to stand by any longer. I've got to try to do something."

"How in the world are you going to feed them?" Manerva asked. "It would take a lot of money and time to run a soup kitchen."

"No, we can't do that. But I found a place where we can get day-old bread for a penny a loaf. We'll buy as much as we can and give one to everybody. That'll keep them from starving. The Lord has impressed on my heart that you can't just *tell* people about the love of God, you've got to prove it by the way you act."

The revival meetings lasted all summer, and the church gave away four to five hundred loaves of bread twice a week. Using this act of love God saved many people and called several into the ministry.

Ben's mother, Jennie, had returned to St. Louis with the Givens. Sixty-two, she only occasionally attended the meetings. During one of them the Holy Spirit fell and people all over the building were slain under His power. Jennie rose from her seat and started toward the door to leave. Suddenly, she was slain by the power of the Holy Spirit, fell to the floor, and spoke in a heavenly language for several hours. She became a great Christian worker and supported Ben and Manerva's ministry for the rest of her life.

Just before the revival closed Ben said, "I don't know what to do about the rest of little Maxine's bill at the funeral home. Everything else is paid off, but I'm even ashamed to tell the undertaker that I'm a preacher, afraid he'll laugh at me for trusting in a God that won't provide for us."

"Yes, I know," Manerva said. "We've always been able to pay our debts. I don't want to leave this one."

They began to fast and pray. In a few days a statement of the balance due came in the mail. In large red letters stamped across the page, it read, "Paid in full for the gospel of Jesus Christ."

They wept tears of thanksgiving and, as a memorial to Maxine, vowed never to charge a fee for weddings or funerals or similar services they might be asked to perform.

On the way back to Lebanon, Ben said, "I think I'm about ready to start pastoring, if God has a place for us. It would be such a blessing to help people the way we did in St. Louis. Not just preaching, but helping in other ways and really getting to know them. Wouldn't it be nice to love a congregation and not have to move on after a few weeks and not ever know what happens to them?"

"Yes, it sure would," Manerva agreed. "Let's start praying about a place. I know He has something special for us."

Pauline said, "I'd like that, too, Daddy. But I'm glad we're going back to Lebanon now so I can graduate from the eighth grade with my friends. I hope we don't move until after that."

"God always takes care of things just the way it ought to be, so we'll pray and leave it in His hands," Manerva responded.

"If we belonged to some organization maybe we could find out about the churches that are available. But I just don't know what to do yet," Ben said.

"Every time you're asked to join you don't seem to want to," Manerva observed.

"I know. I just don't feel right about it. And I'm not going to do something like that until I'm sure it's right and God's in it."

That winter the Givens ministered wherever they were invited. Once, friends south of them, in Wright County, asked them to come hold revival meetings in a place called the Mule Barn. They left Pauline with friends and drove down there. They preached during freezing weather in a building that had the windows broken out, huge cracks in the walls, and a dirt floor.

Persecutions struck again. Almost every night people tied tin cans on herds of goats and ran them through the church during Ben's preaching. Three times a group of young men rode mules through the building from front to back. In spite of the disturbances and discomfort God saved souls.

Several women lived near a community church not far from the Mule Barn and got permission for the revival meetings to move into the church building. Only two other denominations used it on rotating Sundays.

One of the ministers attended their first meeting. Ben asked him to pray. He stepped to the pulpit, waved his hand over it, rebuked the devil, and prayed, "God, don't let this prevailing spirit linger. Amen."

That night a widow, who was a bootlegger and prostitute, gave her heart to the Lord and received the Holy Spirit. She smashed her whiskey still and visited every home in the community apologizing for the life she had lived. God called her to preach, and she became a wonderful blessing to that community for many years.

The Givens ministered at the community church for several weeks. Their only offerings were canned goods and occasionally some fresh meat, when someone butchered a beef or pork.

In the spring, shortly after Pauline finished the eighth grade, Ben received an invitation to hold services in Treece, Kansas, just beyond Joplin. No more talk about how far it was from home; they left on a Sunday morning.

Arriving in Galena, Kansas, some twelve miles from Treece, they had car trouble: a broken timing chain. It was about three o'clock in the morning. The pastor was expecting Ben to begin services that night. Even if a place had been open to buy a chain Ben had only six dollars in his pocket. He walked around the little town until he found a mechanic who lived near his garage.

"I took a timing chain out of a car just like yours about three months ago," he told Ben. "It was worn pretty bad. I threw it out in the trash in the alley. We'll see if it's still there."

They searched for it and found it. The mechanic then cleaned and installed it. He charged Ben six dollars.

Services had already started by the time they reached Treece. Ben went to a side door and asked for the pastor.

"I'm the pastor," the man said. "I guess you want the other one. He left last week after some trouble. I'm just taking over. What can I do for you?"

"I'm Ben Givens, and I'm supposed to preach here tonight. But I need a place to wash up. My hands are greasy from working on my car. Maybe I'll just let it go. My shirt's got grease on it, too, so I'd better just drive on."

"No, come on in. We don't have any place for you to wash, and we have an evangelist here already. But you're welcome to worship with us."

When they went in, hungry, cold, and dirty, the people began to clap. Ben had preached there one Sunday about a year before, and several remembered.

The evangelist asked Ben to preach. He refused. The people clapped and begged. Finally Ben went to the pulpit.

He asked, "How many heard me preach last year?" Hands went up. He continued, "I don't look like I did then. I was clean and didn't have grease on my face, hands, and clothes, and my hair was combed."

The people clapped and laughed. Ben relaxed and preached a message that brought several to the altar for salvation.

Later everyone began to go home. Only the pastor, one other family, and the Givens were left.

The pastor said, “Well, it’s getting late. I guess we might as well turn off the lights and go home.”

The other man asked, “Preacher Givens, do you have a place to stay tonight?”

“No, we don’t. But we’ve got a couple blankets in the car. We could sleep in here if it’s all right. If not, we’ll just sleep in the car.”

“Me and my wife and children are sleeping on the floor over at a man’s house near here. He’s not a Christian but he’s sharing his floor and groceries with us until I can find work. I’m trying to get on at the mine where he works. They pay a dollar a day for ten hours. I’m sure it will be all right if you join us for a night or two.”

“Nervy,” Ben said, “I hate to put you through this.”

“Don’t worry about me, Honey. We’ve got a mansion to live in someday.”

The next morning the man told Ben, “Fellow, I can keep you two or three days, and you are welcome. But find another place as soon as you can.”

That day someone invited the Givens to Tuesday night services in Baxter Springs, about six or seven miles from Treece.

“We’ll take you if you want to go. The church is on Tenth Street. They have good services. Got a good little pastor.”

“We’ll go if you promise not to tell him that we are preachers. We’re too far down on our luck to think about anything but just hearing what somebody else has to say,” Ben said.

“All right, we won’t say a word about it.”

A frail young man with a kind face met them at the door. “I’m Tommy Gale, pastor of the church.”

"We're Ben and Manerva Givens, and this is our daughter, Pauline."

He shook hands with them, then said, "Which one of you is the preacher?"

They looked startled, but both confessed.

"While I was praying and studying today, God told me He was sending two preachers to help us," he said as he handed Ben a Bible. "Brother Givens, God will be with you."

That night the pastor told the congregation, "These are the evangelists we asked God to send our way. The revival is on—"

"Wait a minute," said Ben. "We'll have to pray about this. We can't come here unless we feel it's God's will. Besides, we don't have any place to stay and don't have our things here."

"We'll let you have a room here in the church and fix it up for you, if you'll just preach for us."

"We'll pray about it, then come back in two nights and let you know."

By Thursday night the people had cleaned the room and installed a wood-burning cook stove. Ben told them they would stay. The pastor then asked the people to help furnish the room. He got everything he asked for except a mattress for Ben and Manerva. Ben spoke up, "We can put two benches together and put some quilts on them and make it fine."

From the back of the church an unsaved man called out, "Hey, Preacher, if you promise to bring the mattress to our house when you're done with it, we'll get you one."

The next morning the Sedwick Furniture Company delivered the first innerspring mattress the Givens had ever slept on. The man that furnished it became a Christian during the revival.

Pastor Gale had been seriously ill, and the church asked the Givens if they would become assistant pastors until his health was restored.

"I think we ought to stay," Ben later told Manerva. "Brother Gale might not make it if we don't relieve him of some of the burden. We need the experience, too, before we try to pastor by ourselves. Maybe this is something that will help us and Brother Gale at the same time."

"They can't give us any money, so how will we live?"

"I'll try to find work in the mines around here. If that don't work out, I'll try to pick up whatever I can. We'll make it, if God's with us, and I know He is."

"I don't want you working in the mines. They scare me to death," Manerva said. "What if they cave in or you get TB like your father did? We've had so much trouble the last few years I don't think I can handle any more."

"Hey, hey, little Sweetheart, what's happening to my Nervy? Where's your faith? When we've got God on our side, nothing is too hard. Don't you know that trouble is just opportunity dressed up in overalls?"

For several days Ben searched for work. Although he was in the richest lead and zinc producing center in the world, the mines hired only if someone left, which didn't happen often. He found occasional work in town for about seventy-five cents a day.

One morning Manerva said, "Ben, this is the last bit of flour I have. I'll make bread and gravy with it for our breakfast. We've got nothing else to eat and not one penny to buy anything."

"And not one drop of gas in the car," Ben added.

They had gone to the river the night before for a

baptismal service and the gas ran out just as they reached home. They had coasted into the yard.

Ben walked outside and discovered that all four tires were flat. "Oh, Lord," he prayed, "what am I going to do? The tires are so full of boots they can't be fixed, and I don't even have a spare."

One of the church members, Vic Adams, walked by and stopped to talk.

"Some meeting we've been having, eh?"

"Yes, the Lord has blessed us," Ben replied. "I'm going down to the post office if you'd like to join me."

"Believe I will," Vic answered as he started toward Ben's car.

"No need to go to the car, it's empty and got four flat tires."

"Well, I made a dollar yesterday. If it'll help I'll give you fifty cents of it," Vic offered.

"Thank you, I'm much obliged to you."

Arriving on Main Street they discovered a band from Miami, Oklahoma, marching down the street. Ropes blocked traffic from entering. People lined the street. Ben and Vic found a parked car, sat on its running board, and watched the band strut by.

"Brother Givens! I've been looking everywhere for you," a voice called from behind him.

"Well, praise the Lord, Sister Scott, you've found me," Ben said as he turned.

"Get your car and come up to that grocery store there on the corner as soon as they open the street."

"My car's out of gas and has four flat tires."

"Right there at that store," Mrs. Scott continued as if she hadn't heard Ben. "Somebody, I don't know who, started an offering, a grocery shower, for that preacher down on Tenth Street. That's you, so go get it."

"I'll carry it!" Ben cried out.

"Oh, you can't carry it. You'll need a truck." She handed him some money.

Ben left Vic and started toward home almost running. *I'll borrow Tommy's car,* he thought.

He saw a filling station down on the corner across the street. He noticed the gas priced at nine point nine cents per gallon. *If they've got a can I'll just get some gas and try to pump up the tires enough to last till we get the groceries home. We might not be able to get Tommy's car.*

Just as he started to cross the street, a man came toward him and called, "Preacher, God just spoke to me and said give you some money."

When Ben reached the station he had seven dollars and fifty cents in his pocket.

"Got a can I can get some gas to start my car?" he asked.

"Got a two-gallon one."

"That'll do," Ben said, then noticed two tires lying by the door. After looking them over, he asked, "These tires—are they for sale? They're just right for my car."

"No," the man replied, "they're for that preacher down on Tenth Street."

"That's me!"

"You with Preacher Gale?"

"Yes, sir, I am!"

"Well, then, they're yours. Somebody left them."

"Who?"

"I don't know. Just said they'se for that feller helping out down there."

Ben put the tires around his neck, and with the gas in one hand, started toward home with giant strides.

Manerva saw him coming and ran toward him, "What's the matter?" she called out.

"Nervy, I'm a Pentecostal millionaire!" he told her through his tears.

After he finished the story Manerva said, "Let's not bother Tommy about getting the groceries; let's fix our tires."

They went to work. Before Ben finished pumping up one tire, Manerva started on the next one. They poured the gas into the tank and drove to the grocery store.

They found a large table piled high with everything they needed: eggs, butter, vegetables, fruit, canned food, flour, cornmeal, milk, potatoes, seven kinds of meat, and much more. At home they moved the food into their tiny room, stacking it on the floor, on the chairs, on the table, under the bed, and in any other available spot.

"This morning we didn't have a dust of flour. Now we have everything!" Manerva exclaimed.

They clung together with Pauline between them and prayed thanksgivings to God.

Shortly thereafter, the Diamond Joe Zinc Mine hired Ben to work ten hours a day for one dollar. Every morning he left Manerva crying and praying for his safety.

One day the mine supervisor asked Ben, "You know a David Givens?"

"He was my father."

"I respected that man. I went to work in this mine when I was twelve years old. Your dad was working here and taught me everything I know. He knew all about mines. He'd worked in them for years. I don't think I'd ever got to be the supervisor if it hadn't been for him.

"He knew a lot about preaching, too," the man continued. "Preached every night somewhere. Didn't make any difference where: street corner, brush arbor, anything. All he ever wanted to talk about was God. I heard he got TB and died. That right?"

"Yes, back in '25. He's buried in Phoenix, Arizona."

"Guess you was still living at home when he was here?"

"No, I never knew my father. He and my mother separated when I was very young. I never saw him after that."

"That right? You're a lot like him . . . preaching and all. I heard that after he got TB he just kept right on preaching. Somebody said one time he was up in Joplin and decided to feed everybody that was hungry. The papers announced it, told when and where he was going to do it.

"Now, your old dad didn't have a penny, and didn't care when everybody began to laugh at him. They all thought he was crazy. Just before the day came to feed them, a bunch of merchants, grocery people, I think, got together and decided to cash in on it for the advertisement. They announced in the paper that they was the ones furnishing the food and putting this whole thing on, cooking it and all. Fed more people than they ever thought they could. Helped them merchants, too. Everybody thought they was something great."

"Yes," Ben said, "I've heard about that. Guess he was pretty well-known around here. Lots of people still ask me about him, even though its been almost ten years. Lot of them still coming to church."

"He came from that Parham church here in town, I think," the supervisor said.

"Yes, he did. I've been thinking about going over there to visit the Parhams," Ben said.

"The man that started it all is dead now, but his wife still lives there. He's got some boys, too. I think one's named Wilford."

The day the Givens arrived at Parham's Apostolic Faith Headquarters in Baxter Springs, Wilford and his mother greeted them at the door.

"Any son of David Givens is always welcome here," Mrs. Parham said. "My husband and I had great love and appreciation for him."

They showed the Givens throughout the entire building—originally a brewery. David had helped remodel it into a headquarter's building for the Parham's ministry.

In one bedroom, Mrs. Parham said, "This room was David's. After he restored it we gave it to him. It was always kept empty waiting for him. It's yours now. Any time you want to stay in it you are welcome. If it's occupied when you come we'll move them out and let you have it."

Wilford said, "You know, my father and I were with your father when he died. God told Dad in a vision to go to David Givens in Phoenix, that he was near death.

"When we got there Dad told David that God would give him whatever he wanted, life or death. David said, 'My lungs are gone. I'm old and tired, and I'm worn out and homesick. Pray God will just take the pain away, and that I can go to sleep.' My dad said, 'Brother David, that's a hard prayer, but if that's what you want I'll do it.' We laid hands on him and prayed. When we finished, your dad was gone."

Driving home, Ben said, "You know, I'm not sure I'll ever even catch up with my dad and the work he did, let alone feel like I'm continuing on where he left off."

"Don't say that, Ben Givens," Manerva scolded. We've got years and years of ministry ahead of us, and I feel like we're going to see God move in ways we never thought of. I think we're just getting started. I can't wait to see what He's got for us in the future. I get excited just thinking about it."

13
Ordained

"Ben! Ben!" Manerva called out as soon as he opened the door.

"What's the matter? You look like you're about to be raptured! And what's that you're waving in your hand?"

"It's a twenty dollar bill—that's what it is—a twenty dollar bill! Look at it!"

"I see it. It looks about as big as a bedsheet. But before I can make any sense out of what you're saying you'll have to settle down. Let me get rid of this lunch bucket. Then you start at the beginning and tell me what's happened."

"It's a letter! We got a letter from my sister."

"Which one? You've got a bunch of them."

"Lola, Lola Jones, that's who, from Skellytown. Her husband, Lewis, said you might get work there at the Mobil Oil Company."

"He works for Magnolia, but I think it's the same company," Ben said.

"I don't care what," Manerva continued in one breath, "Lola just said they're building a new gasoline plant there and with your experience you got a good chance of getting on. She sent us this twenty dollar bill to come on. I've been praying all day about it."

"All right, Nervy, if you've been doing the praying, tell me what you found out."

"Well, Brother Gale is a lot better. I'm sure he can handle things here now. I don't feel like we'd be deserting him if we left. Lola said that Skellytown has a few Pentecostal people but they don't have a church of their own to worship in, and we could build one.

"They're all anxious for us to help them. Maybe it's our chance to get started on our own as pastors. I think God put us here to learn before He gives us a place."

She hurried on, "It would be taking a big chance going so far away without any real promise of a job. But if they're hiring, I know you'll get on. Besides, we couldn't be any worse off than we are here. And it would get you out of these awful mines before something bad happens."

"Looks like you've got things pretty well worked out," Ben said with a twinkle. "A man just don't have a chance around here. Let's pray together about it. If we still feel the same way, we'll tell Tommy first and then tell the church. Then we'll leave as soon as we can get ready."

Ben collected a three-dollar check that Friday from the mine, and Monday by daybreak they were headed across Oklahoma, toward the Texas Panhandle and Skellytown.

"I've been thinking about looking into the Assemblies of God. Maybe I'll try to get a preacher's license with them," Ben said during the trip. "I like all I've heard about them. They seem to know what they're doing. And I agree with their doctrine, too, don't you?"

"Yes, I do," Manerva said. "We've met some mighty

fine preachers who are with them. And I keep hearing more and more about them. Maybe this is a good time to look into it."

"We've been by ourselves so much, with no one to back us but kin folks and friends, maybe it's time to do something else," Ben said.

"I think so, too," Manerva said. "Our folks have all stood by us and helped when they could. I'm so thankful for that. But we need to stand on our own now. Just think, every one of our brothers and sisters are saved. Our parents, too. Can you imagine such a thing? I never saw such changes in our families. All except Frank. It's good that he goes to church once in a while with your mother, but that's all he'll do. Maybe before he dies, he'll change."

"I hope so, but we can't make him. It has to come from him. Mom sure did an about-face when she got the Holy Ghost in St. Louis. She's like a different person."

"She *is* a different person," Manerva said. "The Holy Ghost took over her life, and now I have a mother-in-law I'm proud of. God sure changes things, doesn't He?"

Mobil Oil hired Ben to work as an operator for ninety dollars a month. They also gave him a house furnished with gas and electricity. Five years before, Manerva had given up a company home and asked the Lord to help her never let the comforts of a house hold her back and hinder her from His call. Now, once again, she moved into a pretty little company house and found herself mopping floors, cleaning walls, polishing furniture, starching curtains, cooking meals on an immaculate stove, and planting vegetables and flowers.

The Givens immediately associated themselves

with a group of about ten or twelve Pentecostal people worshiping in an abandoned church. Ben applied for and received his minister's license with the Assemblies of God. A short time later, Ben was asked to give up the building they were meeting in, and God moved on Ben's heart to build a new one.

He found three lots available for twenty-five dollars each, but had enough money to buy only two. He bought the lot on either end, hoping no one would want the middle one until he could save money for it. Then he went to the Acme Building Supply and asked for credit.

The owner looked at him and said, "We'll give credit in your name, making you fully responsible for the debt. That's the best we can do. You'll have to take it or leave it."

The Givens prayed for three days and decided to go ahead. After they started building, some grocery store owners drove out to the site. Ben looked up, brushed the sawdust from his overalls, and walked toward them. "Please, Lord," he pleaded, "not trouble again."

Instead of trouble, the men smiled and shook Ben's hand. "Looks like you need some help," one observed.

"Yes, we do, but we can't pay for it. So we're all doing our best, working at night and on Saturdays. It's going to be slow, but we'll make it."

"Preacher," another one spoke, "a lot of idle men are just sitting around and they owe us grocery bills. Work is starting to pick up, and we want to keep our customers. I'll tell you what we'll do. If you can use them, we'll take a dollar a day off their account for each day they work and pay them two dollars a day cash to buy groceries with."

"Thank you! Thank you! We're all much obliged

to you," Ben said as he wiped the sweat from his brow and silently thanked God.

So many men came to work, the site looked like blackbirds on a grainfield. They completed the building in two weeks. The congregation paid the lumber bill in less than one year. They bought the middle lot and paved it for parking. Then they built a three-bedroom parsonage on the third lot.

Shortly after the dedication, in the late spring of 1935, Reverend Thomas, the sectional presbyter, returned from the Texico* District Council meeting and handed Ben his ordination papers.

"What's this?" Ben asked. "I'm not supposed to get these for another year. They told me it'd take two years after I got my license."

"I talked to them about that," Reverend Thomas said. "They looked at your application again. Brother Ralph Riggs from Springfield decided that with your qualifications you should have been ordained last year. It was a pleasure for me to stand in for you at the ordination service."

"I wish I could have been there," Ben said. "I'll do my very best never to bring dishonor to God or the Fellowship."

Skellytown became a school of experience for the Givens family. They plunged into the duties of a pastor, sharing the pulpit equally, counseling, helping, and visiting the congregation, while at the same time working on full-time jobs. Manerva and Pauline opened a restaurant in town. Besides preaching every other sermon, Manerva taught a Sunday school class, played the piano when necessary, and led song services. Along with Pauline she directed the youth. They experienced a strong new sense of belonging.

They became the shepherds Ben longed to be when

so many years before he had looked at the people seated in his first brush arbor and begged God not to let them become sheep without a shepherd.

The Givens continued in Skellytown until 1937. Pauline graduated from high school and married. The Givens then accepted a pastorate in Wellington, Texas, less than twenty miles north of the canyoned banks of the Red River.

---

*At this time New Mexico and West Texas formed a single district, Texico.

14

To Rest Awhile

The church at Wellington had decided to welcome their new pastors by repairing and decorating the entire parsonage. And the ladies collected money from everyone to buy Manerva a dress, shoes, and accessories. They bought Ben a suit, shirt, tie, and shoes. On the night it was presented to them Ben said, "We thank you from the bottom of our hearts. My old suit has been worn so many times it became so familiar to everyone it spoke to them."

Amidst the laughter, contentment, and gladness, tears glistened. The thrill of such love was best expressed and summed up by one elderly gentleman who asked each time Ben wore the outfit, "Pastor, do you like that suit? You know I put fifty cents on buying it for you?"

One day shortly after the Givens moved to Wellington, Manerva got the mail from the box and studied each envelope. "We haven't heard from your brother Ed in quite a while."

"You know, we haven't heard from Mama in a long time, either. Wonder if she's sick or something."

"She said Frank hadn't been feeling too good. Maybe we ought to write again and try to find out if they're all right."

"You'd think Frank would start doing something

about getting right with God before he has a heart attack or something," Ben said.

Ben's thoughts returned to his brother, "I wish Ed had a church to pastor like we have. Holding revival meetings all over is hard on anyone."

"Wouldn't that be nice for him and his family. The people here have been so good to us right from the start. God has blessed us so much. I wish everyone could be as happy as we are."

On April 27, 1939, during the district council meeting of the Assemblies of God held in Lubbock, Texas, Manerva received her ordination papers. She became known as the Holy Ghost preacher. Regardless of the title of her sermon, she somehow always came around to the subject of the Holy Spirit. Her success as an evangelist, as well as copastor, brought many requests for meetings throughout Texas, Oklahoma, and Missouri. But she scheduled her times away from home very carefully and, then, only after much prayer.

Once, she felt definitely led of the Lord to accept an invitation to conduct a revival meeting in Turkey, Texas. One week after the meeting began, a woman, Mrs. Printice Worden, came to Manerva and began to cry.

"I need to talk to you," she said.

"What's the matter?"

"Several years ago the Lord called me to preach, but my husband won't let me. He has fought me ever since. Don't even want me to come to church. He absolutely hates the very thought of a woman preaching and despises every woman who does. I have to tell you something he told me, but my heart is broken. I don't want to tell it because we are having such a wonderful revival.

"My husband is a deputy sheriff and has disturbed and broken up lots of meetings held by women preachers. He told me last night that he is going to deputize two men to sit outside the church and listen. He said, 'If that little preacher gives me an opportunity I'm taking her to jail. If she preaches against sin and hell those two men will bring her in.'

"Please, Sister Givens, go a little easy on sin, so those men will leave you alone. I don't want you hurt by my husband."

"I can't promise that," Manerva said. "God sent me here to lead lost souls to Him. I have to obey Him regardless of the cost. But God is able to keep us, so let's put your husband on the altar right now."

They both knelt at the altar and prayed, "Dear Lord, we know You can take care of this situation according to Your almighty wisdom, so we place Printice Worden in Your hands. We ask that You keep him from disturbing our meeting, and that You save his soul. Help him to understand that You call both men and women to spread the gospel of Jesus Christ."

The meeting lasted two more weeks, without any disturbances from the man. Manerva did not meet him, and no one saw any deputy sheriffs sitting outside.

Manerva's deepest love was pastoring and leading the youth. Oh, how the young people in Wellington loved her! She became both Mama Givens and Dan Cupid to many young men and women who filled the church.

One day Ben teased her, "I declare, Nervy, I never saw anyone loved the way you are. About the only thing those young people will let me do is perform the wedding ceremony after you get them together."

The Givens' great love, their intercessory prayer for lost souls, their daily strength from God, and their knowledge that they were pleasing Him spilled over into the lives around them.

The Givens' most outstanding memory of the four years they spent in Wellington was God calling twenty-one youth from their church into full-time ministry. Ben and Manerva's hearts filled with pride and love as one by one those called into ministry came to them, acknowledging their calling, and asked them to teach them how to preach. The Givens set regular hours to teach them both privately and as a group. Then, they gave one service each week to the candidates, rotating their turn to preach. If one lost his or her sermon or got too scared, the pastors took over.

Often the phone rang at two or three o'clock in the morning, and a voice on the other end anxiously spoke, "I've been studying all night and found a Scripture I don't understand."

The Givens would grab their Bibles and help them. About the time they would get back to sleep the phone would ring again. "I forgot to thank you," the young person would say. "Sorry I needed help and got you up."

Several young people continued their studies at the Shield of Faith Bible College in Amarillo, and many are still in the ministry today.

One cold Saturday morning Manerva entered the house after going to the mailbox and handed Ben a letter, "It's from your brother Ed."

"He'd better have a good explanation for waiting so long to write," Ben said, opening the envelope. "Looks like he's living in Quapaw, Oklahoma, now, from the return."

He read in silence for a moment, then exclaimed, "What in the world is going on? I don't believe what I'm reading."

Manerva began to read along with him. Ed had become acquainted with a traveling team of preachers, who, upon learning of Ed's early divorce from Inez, before he was serving God, convinced him he was living in adultery with his present wife, and that his two children were bastards. "I threw the Bible away and denounced God," he wrote.

Sunday night after the service the Givens climbed into their old Chevrolet and drove through dense fog across Oklahoma to Quapaw. Ed let them know they were unwelcome. It broke their hearts. They prayed, pleaded, and tried to explain the disastrous misinterpretation of the Scriptures. Ed refused to listen. The Givens returned home and made a promise to each other to daily pray for him and his family.

Soon, Ed and his family moved to Kansas City, Kansas. In a short time he wrote Ben his first letter since their visit. The letter read:

> My dear brother and wife,
>
> An evangelist named Ed Slavens [no relation to Manerva] set up a tent close to where we live. We could hear the services. We went and stood outside a few nights. But God got a hook in my jaw, and we sought for forgiveness and reconciliation. He was so wonderful and gave us joy.

Ben and Manerva rejoiced together.

One Sunday afternoon, shortly after, the phone rang. It was Ben's mother. She said, "Frank's had a stroke. The doctor says he might not live."

Once again they left after the evening service, once

again driving across Oklahoma through dense fog, this time to Pawhuska.

Ben and Manerva knelt by Frank's bed and prayed for his salvation and healing. Frank cried and cursed. The Givens prayed until they both began to spit blood.

"Frank," they pleaded, "you've got to confess your sins to God and accept Jesus as your Saviour yourself. We can't do it for you." Frank cried and cursed some more.

Ben left the room and prayed alone, "God, if Frank will get saved I'll ruin my voice praying. If not, relieve me of this burden." Immediately the burden left. He went back into Frank's room; Manerva stood, preparing to leave.

Walking down the corridor, she said, "Ben, I've prayed for God to relieve me of this burden unless Frank would get saved. The burden is gone."

"Sweetheart, I just prayed the same prayer."

They cried together.

Frank recovered from the stroke. The Givens continued to pray that Frank would some day get saved.

For some time Manerva's sister and brother-in-law Ted and Joan Gentry had wanted Manerva and Ben to join them in Sacramento, California. They were undecided until the Gentry's young daughter, June, wrote a letter begging her aunt and uncle to come so she could hear "some good preaching again."

In 1941 the Givens resigned the church in Wellington. They held two revival meetings, one in Fort Worth and one at the Shield of Faith Bible School. They said good-bye to Pauline and her family. (By this time she was living in Houston and had presented her parents with two adored grandchildren, Sandra and Bennie.) Then on April 2, on Ben's birthday, they arrived in Orange Cove, California, where friends had a birthday cake and surprise party for him.

After two weeks of revival meetings in Orange Cove, the Givens moved to Sacramento, near Ted and Joan, where they conducted revival meetings at night and worked in a cannery during the day. Pauline wrote that her husband had asked for a transfer, and they would soon be joining them in Sacramento.

One day Ben said, "We've been preaching a long time. It would be good to rest a while, wouldn't it?"

"Yes," Manerva agreed. "With Pauline and her family on their way out here, I'd like to have a pretty home and time to enjoy our grandchildren. But God called us to preach and we can't forget that."

"We're not going to forget it, Grandma."

"Ben Givens! It's all right for Sandra and little Ben to call me 'Grandma,' but you just stick to 'Nervy.' "

"Yes, ma'am. Nervy, Sweetheart."

"That's better, Grandpa."

"Watch it. I may be nearly fifty years old, but I'm not your grandpa. I have been thinking, though. It's time we started considering what we'll do when we *do* get old. You know preachers can't get social security, and there's no pension fund anywhere for us. Maybe I ought to get a good paying job around here and we'll just preach wherever we can. There's a lot of people that we can preach to right here, and at the same time work somewhere that'll give us a retirement later on."

"Sounds good to me," Manerva agreed. "That'll give me a chance to fix up a beautiful new home the way I've always wanted."

"Wait just a minute. It takes money to buy a house, in case you didn't know."

"Yes, I know. But let's pray about it."

In a few days Ben said, "I met a fellow who's building a big pretty two-story house over on North Avenue. He told me he'd sell it to us if we like it."

The Givens bought the place for two hundred and fifty dollars down and sixteen dollars a month.

They held several revival meetings. Then they bought an abandoned church on the corner of Eleventh and Carmelita Avenue in North Sacramento. They affiliated it with the Assemblies of God and began having regular services.

Ben enrolled in Sacramento Junior College, taking special training to become an aircraft engine mechanic. He graduated with honors and applied for a job at McClellan Air Force Base (ten miles northeast of Sacramento).

One Sunday before his job approval came through, he, Manerva, and Joan took an afternoon drive through the Fair Oaks section of Sacramento. They saw a man with his truck backed up to a new house, trying to unload furniture and kitchen appliances.

Ben slowed and asked, "Need some help?"

"Yes, I do. Thank you," the man replied.

Ben removed his coat and went to work. After the job was finished the man said, "Let's have a beer."

"Thank you, but I don't drink."

"How about a cigarette?"

"I don't smoke either."

"What kind of man are you?"

"I'm a Pentecostal preacher. I ministered this morning in town and was just passing by when I saw you needed help."

"You mean you are a preacher and you were willing to get grease and dirt all over your hands and shirt sleeves?"

"Grease and dirt don't hurt me. I worked for years in the Texas oil fields. Let me introduce myself, I'm Ben Givens, and this is my wife, Manerva, and her sister Joan."

"Pleased to meet you," he said. Then he gave Ben a puzzled look, "Fellow, you are a real captain!"

"Thank you. Well, if I've helped you all I can, guess we'll be going."

"Goody-bye, Captain," the man called out.

That October, McClellan Air Force Base hired Ben to work in the Third Wing Engine Department. Two days later he was disassembling a greasy engine and preparing it to be cleaned. During the afternoon a man walked by, and Ben spoke to him.

"Who was that man that just went by?" he asked the foreman.

"He's the Third Wing superintendent," the foreman replied. "Why?"

"I've seen him some place, but don't remember where."

In a day or two the superintendent walked over to Ben and said, "The foreman said you think you might know me."

"Yes, you look familiar to me. I'm a preacher and see a lot of people. I can't always remember everyone."

The superintendent looked at Ben a moment, smiled, and said, "Hey, Old Captain, you're the preacher that helped me unload my furniture."

Ben shook hands after wiping the grease from his hands.

"You sure aren't afraid to get dirty grease all over you, are you?"

"No, it goes with the job."

A few days later the superintendent moved Ben

to a clean job. Two weeks later Ben was transferred to the bearing department, inspecting bearings. After one month he was sent to the test block to inspect rebuilt engines. A short time later he was put in charge of its shift and crew.

Ben continued to receive promotions and pay raises. By 1943 he was in charge of final check inspection at the test block. His skill and knowledge in the field of mechanics helped him achieve this responsible position and made him a valuable employee.

Ben liked his job. He had a retirement plan that included the years he spent in the Army. His salary enabled him to make three or four house payments each month. Soon, for the first time in their lives, they would own their home.

Not long after Pauline and her family moved from Texas to California, another grandson, Thomas, found his way into the world and hearts of the Givens family.

Starched curtains, clean walls, waxed floors, and polished furniture adorned Manerva's beautiful new home. Flower beds, fresh-cut lawn, and a hearty vegetable garden embraced the friendly house. The tantalizing smell of cookies, bread, and fine food greeted friends, neighbors, and relatives, especially grandchildren.

The Givens resigned the church, and occasionally ministered as guests in neighboring churches. After services one night two ladies asked Ben and Manerva, "Are you the Givens who were in South West City, Missouri, in 1931?"

"Yes, we are. Were you there?"

"We are the two ladies you took home one night and were greeted by my husband's cursing and threat to kill you. He even grabbed my Bible and tore it to pieces right there in front of you. Do you remember us?"

"Indeed we do remember you! How wonderful to see you again after all these years. Where is your husband? Is he here?"

"No, he's not here. He spent several years in the state insane asylum and recently died there."

"I'm so sorry to hear that. Where is your daughter now, the one I baptized after your husband said he would drown both of us?"

"She's married, and she and her husband are missionaries."

"Well, praise the Lord!"

Ben and Manerva Givens in 1938, while pastoring in Wellington, Texas

Ben baptizing his daughter, Pauline

15
Live Oak

Manerva handed Ben the phone, "It's Brother Thurmond from Santa Cruz. Wants to talk to you."

"Brother Givens, don't you think it's about time you and your wife started pastoring again?" Reverend R. J. Thurmond, Northern California and Nevada District Secretary, asked.

"We're doing all right. We preach some in this area on Sundays and once in a while hold a meeting."

"I know, but we've got a church that needs a new pastor and I thought you might be interested."

"I don't think so, but where is it?"

"A little town called Live Oak, about forty-five or fifty miles north of Sacramento. Why don't you just drive up there Sunday and preach for them? Then you can decide about it."

"We'll go preach, but I don't think we're interested in pastoring. I'm real happy with my job here, and we've got to think about putting something away for our old age."

"You pray about it. I'll call one of the deacons up there and tell him you'll be there Sunday."

It was mid-February 1943. World War II shrouded the nation, forcing shortages and government rationing of many essentials. The Givens used most of their gas ration coupons to get to Live Oak.

"You'll have to ride to work with someone all next week," Manerva said.

"I'll call one of the fellows I work with."

The town of about one thousand residents quietly sat in the middle of rich farming land. Almond orchards were beginning to bloom. But peach, prune, plum, walnut, pear, and other trees rested dormant and bleak in their muddy, rain-soaked orchards. Open land lay blackened from rice stubble burning.

"Not very pretty country," said Ben.

"Can't judge it now, with everything so dead-looking. Look how the almond orchards brighten things up." Manerva tried to be positive.

They joined the adult Sunday school class in the sanctuary. Ben watched as the secretary changed the figures on the Sunday school record posted on the wall behind the pulpit: Present Today—52.

On the way home Ben asked, "What do you think?"

"Awfully nice people."

"Yes, mostly midwesterners like us, I think."

"I liked the pianist."

"I met her husband. I got the feeling from the way he talked that they like to hunt and fish about as much as we do."

"Made me want to pastor again," Manerva said.

"Me too. God's been talking to me about it."

"I don't know. I'd hate to give up what we have."

"I don't think I want to either," said Ben. "God gave us that job, helped us get a new house just before the war stopped all the building, and we're settled now. We don't have to give up preaching just because I work on a good job."

In their prayer that night they told God if He wanted them to go to Live Oak a unanimous vote would tell them and they would obey Him regardless of the sacrifice.

The next morning at work the dispatcher walked up to Ben. "Givens," he said, "report to the chief."

Ben opened the office door and stepped in.

"Hey, Ben. What goes on here?"

"What do you mean?"

"Three months is the limit on how often you can receive promotions."

"Yes, that's right," Ben agreed.

The chief looked at the papers he held. "I see here that less than three months ago you got two promotions about a month apart and another one last week. Now another promotion just came through for you, effective the first of March. You must be doing something right around here."

Ben thought for a minute, then said, "All I know is that I wrote a letter outlining all the procedures in final inspection and sent it to headquarters in Patterson Field, Ohio, like we're required to do."

"Guess that's what brought in this last promotion. I know one thing, I've never seen anyone work as hard as you do and learn as fast as you have. Keep up the good work. You're the kind we like to keep a long time."

"Thank you, sir, I'm much obliged to you."

After Ben told Manerva about the promotion and raise they went to prayer again.

"Lord, there are so many preachers who could pastor Live Oak just as good, and a lot better, than we can. We'll pray every day that just the right one will come along."

Their prayers seemed to hit the ceiling and drop off. They continued praying, telling God how to run His Live Oak affairs. Finally after many hours, their hearts broke and they wept repentance before Him. They put their arms around each other and sobbed to the God they loved, "We know You can take care of us in our old days as well as You take care of us now. We would rather serve You and be in Your will than to have a mansion and all the riches of this earth. We'll go where You want us to go, and do what You want us to do."

Tuesday, Rev. Thurmond came by on his way to Live Oak to conduct the business meeting.

"What is your decision?" he asked.

"We've decided if we get a unanimous call, we will go."

About 11 P.M. the phone rang.

"Ben," Brother Thurmond said, "you and your wife are pastors at Live Oak."

There was silence.

"Are you awake, Ben?" he asked.

"Yes, but it'll take thirty days to get a release from my job. I guess we can drive back and forth if we get the gas."

The next Sunday the Givens accepted the pastorate and inspected the parsonage, which sat next to the church.

"It'll hold only about half of our furniture," said Manerva.

"Give some of it away, sell some, and store the rest," Ben suggested.

"We'll have to live real careful. They said the finances were low, and we only get a percent of that," Manerva said.

"Haven't we always lived careful?"

Before moving, Manerva prayed, "Lord, I almost failed You because I wasn't willing to leave this house. You know it's the most beautiful home I've ever lived in, and Ben's job is the best he's ever had. Forgive me for loving what I can see, and forgetting Your unseen riches. Forgive me for hanging onto the things of this world more than Your precious call on our lives. I know there is a mansion waiting for me if I remain faithful. I know that I'll live forever in that beautiful place not made by hands."

The day after they moved, Ben joined Manerva in the kitchen. "Our hot water tank hasn't got a shut-off. We'll have to turn it on and off when we use it or it will blow up in our face," he told her.

"Don't come telling me any more troubles. I'm having enough right now trying to figure out what's smelling so bad around this kitchen sink."

Ben got down on his knees to take a look. Manerva knelt beside him. "Look here," Ben said. "This drain pipe is an old Model T Ford exhaust pipe and it runs the water right out on the ground under the floor. No wonder it stinks."

"Guess that's also the reason the rats are so healthy around here."

"That's not the only reason. Those restrooms out back of the church are part of that problem. I think I'll start fixing up the plumbing before I do anything else," Ben decided. "Maybe I can find a better hot water tank somewhere and pipes to get all the water into the septic tank. I want to get the restrooms moved into the church somehow."

"Where you going to get all that stuff now?" asked Manerva. "You know you can't buy anything like that till the war's over."

"I'll look around and see if I can find some used things. There ought to be something around somewhere."

The work began. Ben helped Manerva at night

after work and on Saturdays. Before a week was over the place started to take on a new look. At the same time the spiritual needs of the people did not go neglected.

Ben came in one Saturday from town and said, "Sweetheart, there's Pentecostal people scattered all over this community. They've come here from back east like we thought, to work wherever they can find anything. They're just not going to church anywhere. Some seem to be in pretty bad shape financially. There's not much work in the winter, so they have to save what they can in the summer to get them by till the next season."

"Ben, I feel like we're going to be able to help them. I feel so good about being here."

The people had come from miles around to hear the new pastors. Families came, packing the building. Sunday school classes were held outside under walnut trees. Word had spread quickly in the early spring, during the peach thinning time when many worked together in the fields.

On July 11, 1943, five months after the Givens accepted the pastorate, the Sunday school secretary changed the figures on the record to read: Present Today—318!

Often in the dead hours of the night God's hand "shook" Ben and Manerva to get up and pray for a troubled family. Sleepy-eyed they would obey the Spirit. "Oh, God," they prayed, "give us the wisdom to help these dear, lonely people."

The church's weekly offerings were less than ten dollars the first ten weeks the Givens pastored. Ben continued his job at McClellan Air Force Base for thirty days. Then they lived on accumulated vacation pay. By the fourteenth week the offering was fifty-two dollars. After that time they were well cared for.

Many times after spotting someone in the worship service who was in need, Ben and Manerva slipped their entire week's allowance into thankful hands. No one else ever knew.

They began to hear, "We're putting away a little now and then, and when we find something we can buy we might just buy a place here. It'd be cheaper than renting. If we could get lumber, we'd just build us a little place. Land's not so high here, and we could get by cheaper doing it ourselves."

The Givens helped many find land, helped them find lumber (mostly used), helped them find jobs; they canned fruit and vegetables with them, took fresh pies and homemade chicken and dumplings to them after long days in the field.

Ben and Manerva came alive—full of joy, grace, fascination, strength, and drive. Their hearts burned with the fire of God's anointing. Manerva taught Sunday school in one of the expansions they had built onto the sanctuary. Folding doors separated them from the main section. Many times God's Spirit fell on the class, and they worshiped God. When the doors were opened at eleven o'clock the praise and worship spread to the entire congregation.

The youth loved and befriended each other and "ran in packs" at school and everywhere. But most of all they prayed for each other, often until the early hours of the morning, until one received salvation, or the Holy Spirit, or, simply, relief from a burden. They welcomed newcomers and learned compassion for souls from the example of their leaders.

"Ben, who is that pretty young girl that just came in?" Manerva asked one Sunday morning.

"I don't know, but let's go find out. She looks lonesome and a little scared."

They walked toward the back of the church and took the young woman's hand.

"We're the pastors, Brother and Sister Givens."

"Hello," she said, "I'm Maxine Deaton. I heard there was a lot of young people here and I'd like to get to know them. I'm kinda lonesome out here all by myself."

"Oh, Honey," Manerva cried as she hugged her. "Our little girl that we lost was named Maxine. *You* can be our Maxine now. Do you live close by?"

"Not too far. My folks went back to Arkansas after the fruit season, but I decided to stay here. I've got a job at Montgomery Ward in Marysville, and I didn't want to leave it. There's nothing much to do back in Arkansas."

"You mean you're living all by yourself? No wonder you're lonesome. After church we'd like for you to come over and eat with us. But first let's get you acquainted with some of the young people around here."

Maxine became another of the Givens many spiritual children. They led her to the Lord and to the baptism in the Holy Spirit, gave her a Bible (her first), introduced her to all the youth, and loved her. She returned their love. Later, Maxine married J. T. Long, one of the young people in the church.

At Live Oak there was a time for preaching, a time for praying, a time for gathering, a time for weeping, and a time for fun.

Soon after the Givens arrived in Live Oak, Guy Finley asked, "You two like to go hunting and fishing?"

"That's our greatest weakness. We'd rather go out

in the woods and hunt and fish than eat when we're hungry."

"We like to go, too, and we've been wishing we had somebody to take with us. We've got some pretty good places staked out up in the Sierras. Let's get together during deer hunting season. You've been working long and hard, and it's about time you took a break."

That was the beginning of many church buck stews. Ben and Manerva seldom missed their target. They always shared their good fortune with the church. The Finleys and many others also shared and joined in the winter celebrations. One year they rented the Grange hall in town and fed two hundred and fifty people.

This was also the beginning of a lifetime friendship with the Finleys, adding to the long list of people the Givens cherished.

Later the two couples built a hunting cabin in the mountains and dedicated it to the service of God, and shared it with their friends and relatives. Once a young boy got lost in the woods near the cabin. The sheriff opened the cabin for the posse and later thanked the Givens and the Finleys for its use and promised to replenish the supplies used. The young boy's mother wrote and thanked them also.

Sometimes Ben took a bunch of boys from the church on fishing trips. They camped out, had fireside services, and made dedications to God. Manerva and the girls would have sleepouts. Ben was always drafted to be the watchdog. Then, in the morning, what a time flipping hot cakes! Those dainty, pretty, light eaters would eat like shoveling coal into a locomotive engine.

Both the youth and the Givens enjoyed playing

jokes on each other. One Sunday night after services Ben and Manerva were in bed, and the phone rang. "Is this Reverend and Mrs. Givens?" the voice asked.

"Yes."

"Well, we're from Wellington, Texas, and want to come over and say hello."

Ben and Manerva jumped out of bed, dressed, and straightened up the house. Then the phone rang again, "Sorry we can't come over," the voice said and hung up.

At that moment the front door opened and about twenty or twenty-five young people came in, went to the refrigerator, cleaned it out, visited a while, then paraded over to the Finleys.

Just as in Wellington, Nervy played Dan Cupid, and Ben performed many wedding ceremonies for the young people. One of the last jokes the youth pulled on Ben was about fifteen years after the Givens resigned the church.

A young man said to Ben, "Brother Givens, a bunch of us fellows you married are getting together for a party. We want you to join us."

"Thanks, I would be delighted," Ben said.

The young man said the party would be down on the banks of the Feather River.

"We've found a big tree and have a new rope. It's going to be a hanging party, and you are the victim."

That's the only time Ben "failed" his young people: He felt an urgent call out of town that night and his absence broke up the party.

Not only were Ben and Manerva loved and respected by their congregation, but the entire community respected their wisdom and leadership. In 1947 Ben was asked to become a member of Live Oak's first board of councilmen when the community called a special election and voted to incorporate and become a city. A few months later, in the general election, Ben was made Live Oak's first elected mayor. He received congratulations from Governor Earl Warren and was given membership in the California Peace Officers Association. After a short time, however, Ben resigned, fearing this community service might take him from his labor for God and His people. The true desire of Ben's heart was to shepherd the flock God had entrusted to him.

By 1947 the Live Oak congregation filled the church building and three expansions that had been added to the church. The people had reached a settling, a contentment, a plateau of living. The devastating effect of the Great Depression and World War II had eased, and the people rested. Ben and Manerva began to pray that the congregation would not drift into indifference and unconcern.

In March, during a Bible lesson that Ben taught, he mentioned the one hundred and twenty who tarried in the Upper Room until the Holy Spirit fell. An elderly man commented, "I wonder what would happen today if we had a prayer meeting that went for ten days?"

Later, a woman in the church announced that her home would be open day and night for ten days of continual prayer. People were invited to come and stay as long as they could. There would be no talking or entertaining, only prayer. The Lord impressed on her that He had ordered this, and the Holy Spirit was the host.

The meeting began on a Friday night. Several people were there at all times, with prayers going up continually. The Lord began to stir the people. It was a time of renewal and of meeting needs. Many were healed. Some were called into the ministry. Others rededicated their lives to God.

Throughout the entire time, day and night, far too many were touched by God to mention individually. But one day an unsaved man drove into the yard and later told Ben "the air all around that house was aflame with the Spirit of God."

The meeting continued throughout the next week and ended on Saturday night at midnight. The next morning people packed the church and filled the yard. They stood at all the windows trying to see and hear what God had done. Great rejoicing and praise went up to God as people stood in line to tell what had happened to them during the prayer meeting.

The service continued without a break until four-thirty. In the afternoon others came from nearby churches to listen and rejoice. Even after the break some remained at the church praying and worshiping until the evening services began. The glory of God came down in deluges. Revival began. Many said, "This is the most miraculous day of my life!"

It was a time of great fellowship, of great expectations, of great spiritual concern, of great unity, of great times of God's blessing and outpouring of the Holy Spirit. The Givens never forgot the way God moved on the people.

In the weeks that followed, the people's love for each other was renewed, and they reached out to everyone in one accord. Souls were saved. Often the services lasted until seven o'clock the next morning, with many leaving the church to go to work. No one would stay at home on church night for fear they would miss something.

The blessings of God began to flow to the towns nearby. Manerva took some of the youth who were called to preach and went to several nearby communities, such as Biggs, Olivehurst, and Sutter, and helped establish churches. She also held revival meetings throughout northern California.

In 1948 the Givens, along with several neighboring pastors, organized the first camp meeting of the Northern California/Nevada District's Butte Section. It was held at Long Lane, near Sterling City, high in the Sierras. Reverend W. T. Gaston was their first camp speaker.

Two years later Reverend Everett Morgan, pastor at Red Bluff, mentioned that government land was available in Lassen Volcanic National Park. Ben and Manerva contacted other pastors about the property and set a date to look it over. Everett Morgan, Albert Rowley, M. M. York, Kenneth Carney, Charles Elmes, Ben Givens, and their wives met there, spread a picnic lunch, and discussed the possibilities. That afternoon they prayed. Then they walked completely around what is now Lassen Assemblies of God Campground.

The churches began to cooperate and donate time, money, and labor. Truckloads of men and boys came to clear trees and brush, dig a well, and build restrooms. Ben's sixteen-foot vacation trailer became their camp office. His 1937 Chevrolet was the first camp car. Guy Finley gave them a Chevrolet one-ton truck. They hung gasoline lanterns and began services with Reverend Lewis Hoff as evangelist. Reverend Charles Elmes became the first camp manager.

Now the camp is modern, comfortable, and considered one of the best in the nation. It is used for different activities by the churches—youth camps, senior citizens camps, etc.—and every July it is packed to capacity for another refreshing old-fashioned camp meeting.

In September 1951, after eight years of successful ministry in Live Oak, Ben and Manerva felt led of the Lord to resign and take the pastorate in Delhi, California.

But before they left they bought a small home in Live Oak to keep for their retirement years.

Manerva told Ben, "This is where I want to live when we get old. It's home."

"Yes," Ben replied. "We may wander around for a lot of years, but this is where I want to come home. God turned a tub of honey over in our souls here and made us feel as much at home as He did for so many others. He gathered us up in His arms and loved us too, just as He gathered them up in His arms and loved them."

16

The Sheriff From Turkey, Texas

"Stop the car!" Manerva cried out. "Something's wrong with Ben!"

It was October 1955. Ben and Manerva were on their way to Barstow from Herlong, California, with some friends.

"What's the matter, Ben?" Manerva called to him as they laid him on a blanket along the roadside.

A deep, daggerlike pain struck Ben in his left shoulder. Manerva's voice faded away. He seemed to be slipping into a dark cone-shaped chasm.

Ben soon regained consciousness but could hardly speak, and his left arm and foot hung helpless. He was sent, under protest, to the veteran's hospital in Reno, Nevada. He had suffered a heart attack.

Ben told the nurse, "Son, I don't belong here. God has healed me. I'm a preacher, and I want to get out of here so I can get on with my business."

"Preacher," the young man said, "I don't believe in God, and you look too smart to believe that bilge."

Ben began to witness to the nurse, telling how God had delivered him from sinful habits and forgiven his deplorable sins. The nurse listened and asked questions. Each day he returned to hear more about God, but never made a confession in Ben's presence.

"Ben," the nurse said one day, "there's an old man

down the hall dying unsaved and alone. You ought to go see if you can help him. He needs God. We're not supposed to allow any missionary work here, but I'll take you down there in your wheelchair, and you do what you can. I won't let anyone know what you're doing."

Ben led the old soldier to God. Then he called the man's estranged wife and daughter. They visited him, and he asked their forgiveness. They made peace with each other and rejoiced in the joy of the Lord. The old man died the next day.

After that the nurse wheeled Ben around into many of the rooms and wards. Ben led several Army veterans to the Lord before he was discharged, three weeks later. He was completely well.

"I know now why God let this attack hit me. Those old men needed someone to tell them how to get saved before they meet their Maker."

The doctor advised Ben to resign his church and seek employment that would be less stressful. They were pastoring the Assemblies of God church in Herlong. Ben served as presbyter of the Lassen Plumas Section of the Northern California/Nevada District and traveled much throughout the Sierra Mountains. The Givens had gone to Herlong after a successful and happy pastorate in Delhi.

Ben took the doctor's advice, and he and Manerva moved to their home in Live Oak. But soon the Lord dealt with them about pastoring again.

In March 1956 they accepted the church in Reno, Nevada, where only eighty-six people attended Sunday school the first Sunday. Ben and Manerva found the church deeply in debt and unable to pay its monthly bills. They began to pray.

Ben called a business meeting and told the people

that he and Manerva would allow them to reduce their weekly salary by one third.

"I trust that all of you will also sacrifice for a while."

In six months the people had paid all the outstanding bills and returned the pastor's salary to what it had previously been. They made some improvements on the building and had a mortgage burning service fourteen months before the final payment of the mortgage was due. The average attendance of the Sunday school had almost doubled, having risen to one hundred sixty.

One Sunday afternoon the phone rang. Ben answered.

"I'm Reverend Printice Worden," the voice spoke.

"Your name is not familiar. Do I know you?" Ben said.

"No, not exactly. But your wife does. Could I speak to her?"

Manerva took the phone.

"I'm Reverend Printice Worden. You should know me, I'm that old mean sheriff from Turkey, Texas, who threatened to close down your meetings."

"You a preacher?"

"Yes. I'm here for a few days and would like to come to your church tonight if that's all right."

"Yes, of course it's all right." They talked for a few more minutes. Then Manerva said, "It's my night to preach, and I'd like to ask you to take my place if you will."

"I'd be happy to."

Just before the evening services started, Printice Worden arrived at the church. Manerva almost fainted when she saw him. His entire nose was gone! There was only a hole in his face about the size of a silver dollar. She began to cry and turned her face away from him.

That night Worden told the congregation, "I knew your pastor's wife in Turkey, Texas. She held a revival there many years ago. I was a deputy sheriff and tried to disturb the services. I hated women preachers and even threatened her.

"This affliction I have on my face appeared soon after her revival ended. It came as a little sore inside my nose. It wouldn't heal, so I went to a doctor. After much treatment he decided to send me to the Mayo Clinic. They diagnosed it as cancer and said they couldn't do anything for me. 'Go home,' they advised, 'and set your house in order. You don't have long to live.'

"I sent for my wife to come after me, and she brought her pastor and his wife to help drive. Riding in the car, I spotted a nice shady placed and asked them to stop. 'Right under that large tree is where I'm going to give my heart to God and ask forgiveness for my sins,' I told them. I cried and repented. God forgave me, blessed me, filled me with the Holy Ghost, called me to preach, and healed my cancer all at the same time.

"But my nose was already gone, and God did not restore it. I have to suffer this because I wouldn't let my wife preach, and I persecuted Sister Givens and all other women preachers who came to our town.

"Once we saved enough money for plastic surgery, but my wife became ill, so we spent the money on her surgery. God spoke to my heart that this is my punishment for being such a bigot.

"I never wanted to see anyone so bad in all my life as I did Sister Givens. I want to ask her forgiveness in front of all of you for the wrong I did. I also want to tell her that my wife travels with me whenever she can and preaches with me.

"I would like to ask all of you to pray that somehow God will allow me to have plastic surgery before I die."

Ben and Manerva prayed faithfully for the Wordens. About twenty years later they received word that Reverend Worden had died without ever having facial surgery.

17

"I Want To Preach"

In 1960 Ben and Manerva resigned the church in Reno and moved back to Live Oak to rest and be near his mother, Jennie, who was ninety years old. Jennie had moved there in 1949, shortly after Ben's stepfather, Frank, died.

"Did he ever ask God to forgive him?" Ben had quickly asked when his mother called to tell him of Frank's death.

"No, not that I know of," she replied.

When Jennie arrived in Live Oak, she said, "All I have left to live for is God. I want to spend the rest of my life witnessing and helping those God sends my way."

Just before Jennie's death on December 27, 1961, two months before her ninety-second birthday, she said, "I don't know why God has let me live so long. I'm tired of living in this world and long to go home to be with my Lord. But there is a reason. Maybe there is one more person somewhere that I must witness to."

She, along with Ben and Manerva, had become one of thirteen charter members of Tierra Buena–Calvary Temple in Yuba City, just nine miles south of Live Oak.

The young pastor and his wife, Marvin and Louise

Long, had started the work only after many hours in prayer and counsel with the Givens.

Ben said, "Son, we believe God is in this. Go, and give it your very best. We will support you, help you with the building, and never cease to pray for God's blessing on this endeavor."

Marvin and Louise had been saved, filled with the Holy Spirit, married, and called to preach under the Givens' ministry in Live Oak. They became two more of their "adopted children."

But after Calvary Temple became established, the Longs couldn't keep Ben and Manerva still. Although in their sixties, they held revivals in many parts of California, Oregon, Texas, Oklahoma, Missouri, and Kansas.

While in Kansas they visited Ben's brother, Ed, who had cancer. He had lived a dedicated Christian life for many years.

One day in August 1965, a short time after Ben and Manerva's visit, Ed took the doctor's hand and said, "I want to thank you and all those who have taken care of me. But, Doc, just one thing bothers me. I am ready to meet God. But I guess I won't be meeting you in glory."

The doctor began to cry and hugged him. He said, "Ed, I love and serve your God, and I promise to see you later. God bless you."

That was Ed's last testimony.

Ben and Manerva decided to go to Idaho and visit Manerva's brother-in-law and his new bride, Mary. (Joan had died several years before.) While there, the Givens became acquainted with Mr. and Mrs. John Gillihan who owned and managed a hunting guide service in the wilderness of Idaho, near Yellow Pine, in the central part of the state.

Mrs. Gillihan became ill and Manerva and Mary Gentry took her to the hospital in McCall, fifty miles away, where she remained for surgery. They returned to the Gillihan home, took care of the three children, and operated the boarding house for the hunters until Mrs. Gillihan recovered.

Ben and Manerva started a children's revival in Yellow Pine, in a building where Sunday school classes were held each Sunday. At the end of the revival Ben baptized sixteen people (of which some were adults) in the Salmon River, properly called the Ice Hole.

One day John Gillihan asked Ben, "Would you help me out a little? I've got a group of hunters up at Bismark Camp without a cook, and I can't find one to send. Would you go up there and cook for them while I try to find one?"

"I'll be glad to go," Ben said. "I can use some of my old Army cooking skills."

"I'll have to warn you, though—they drink, fight, and are generally pretty vulgar. And they're pretty well-to-do. It took two mules just to pack in their booze."

"Don't worry about me, I've handled that kind before."

Ben found two tents set up: one for the kitchen with the cook's bed in the corner and the other for sleeping the hunters.

"Men," Ben explained, "I'm a Pentecostal preacher, and I love to have good clean fun. But I won't drink your booze, I won't enter into vulgarity and fights, and I won't smoke your cigars and cigarettes. You can do as you please, but I ask that you also allow me to do as I please."

They agreed.

The first night, Ben served supper, washed the dishes, and began preparing the breakfast menu.

"Hey, Preacher, how about playing poker with us, just for fun? No money on the table."

"No, thank you."

The men made coffee, grabbed a bottle of wine, gathered around the kitchen table, and the game was on. Ben hung a gasoline lantern over his bed and began to read the Bible.

About an hour later one of the hunters turned to Ben and asked, "Why don't you talk to us about the Bible?"

Ben eagerly rolled out of bed and thanked the men. "Is there any certain Scripture you would like to hear?"

"No, you choose."

He read Matthew 16:18: "Upon this rock I will build my church; and the gates of hell shall not prevail against it." Then he talked for about half an hour.

Every night for ten nights it was poker, wine, and talk on the Bible. Ben used the same Scripture each time.

After they returned to base camp, John looked over their supplies. Surprised, he asked, "Hey, fellows, did Ben convert all of you? You brought back nearly all your booze."

"I'll tell you what," one answered, "if you'll get Ben to be our cook next year, we'll pay our full dues right now."

Ben returned each year during hunting season for the next five years. Many times Manerva went with him to the campsites. They witnessed to all the hunters.

Several men having marital problems asked for

counsel. One was Pentecostal, but had turned away from God. The Givens prayed for him and his family. When he returned home his family was reconciled, and they joined an Assemblies of God church.

One man hunted four hours the first day and spent the remainder of his time talking and praying with Manerva. He said, "This trip cost me seven hundred and fifty dollars, but it's worth a lot more than that if I can just have my home and family back together again."

Once Ben went to East Fork Camp without Manerva and met five men from Washington, D.C.

"So you're a preacher?"

"Yes, and very proud of it."

The camp was equipped with a phone. Soon after they arrived it rang.

"Telephone, telegraph, tell a woman. We thought we were in primitive country."

One said, "I sent my old bag to Japan."

Another said, "I sent mine to her mother's."

Another remarked, "I gave mine five hundred dollars and told her to hoof it, that I didn't care what she did."

One said, "I sent mine to Florida."

They all agreed that this was to be a month of freedom.

"Ben, you married?" one finally asked.

He firmly responded, "Yes, I am happily married and wish she could be here right now. I'm lonesome for her when we are apart for just one day. I want to tell you men when you refer to my wife before me you call her the Lady, or Mrs. Givens. I resent any off-color remarks. We have been together over forty years and grow happier every year."

A few mornings later the handle on a pot of boiling

water that Ben was carrying broke and spilled the water down the front of Ben's clothes. He screamed in pain and began to pray. His skin was angry red. Being without medical supplies the men wanted him to ride a horse to the base camp for help.

"Fellows," Ben said, "it's fourteen miles to the base. And, besides, I belong to God. He will take care of me."

The men went hunting but they returned in about three hours.

"We want to look at your stomach and legs," they said.

The burns had completely healed.

The men didn't drink anymore but listened as Ben told them about God.

They corresponded with him and Manerva for many years after that.

Not only did the Givens minister to the hunters, but they held revivals in Yellow Pine and the surrounding areas, many remote and wooded.

Each year the Givens returned, pulling a utility trailer filled with used clothing and canned goods for the people living in the isolated areas. Pauline, Calvary Temple, and friends in Live Oak kept them in supplies.

They were called many names by the people in Idaho: cooks, hunters, witnesses for Christ, and, when they told some big hunting story, they were called storytellers. But their favorite and most cherished name of all was preachers.

One Sunday night in McCall, Manerva preached in the evening services and eleven people were saved.

"Just like the early days when we used to preach in the woods of Missouri," she told Ben. "Now we don't preach to bootleggers, but to booze drinkers, and souls just as troubled. People are always the same, any time, any place. Whether they are rich or poor, whether they buy their whiskey or make it, they all need someone to tell them about God. We've hung many gasoline lanterns in schoolhouses and other buildings, and preached to hungry souls, just as we are doing now."

"Well, we haven't had to build any brush arbors in Idaho," Ben said. "Not yet, anyway. And I've not made any cigar box pulpits."

"Oh, I wouldn't mind if we did. I feel like I could use that old crosscut saw right now just as easy as I did when we were young," Manerva said.

"You probably could. Not too many seventy-year-old women could ride a horse all over these Idaho hills like you've been doing."

"Oh, what wonderful memories we have," Manerva said. "Do you suppose we are getting old? I don't feel like it. We don't seem to be slowing our pace any."

But Reverend and Mrs. Benjamin Givens did slowly, ever so slowly, ease their pace. However, they never lost that beauty that comes from delighting in the love of God. And they never lost their beautiful sense of humor nor did they stop serving others. They were faithful to Tierra Buena–Calvary Temple, seldom absent from the services. They attended with prayers, support, and sensitivity.

An old friend, Reverend Bill Popejoy from Belton, Missouri, conducted several prophecy meetings in Calvary Temple before his death. One day he and Manerva had a friendly argument about the mansions in heaven. He said that the word "mansion" in John 14:2 was mistranslated and should read "places."

Manerva told him, "No, you're wrong. My Lord promised me that if I was faithful I'd have a beautiful mansion to live in, and I believe I will."

Manerva Givens preached her last sermon on Mother's Day, 1982. She told the young wives to be a good companion to their husbands and always encourage and help them. Her words of wisdom were mixed with fun and laughter. She used light humor to illustrate profound truths. During the message she laughed and said, "You know why God made Eve, don't you? Because Adam couldn't find his socks."

Sunday, November 14, 1982, the Givens left Calvary Temple after the morning services.

Ben said, "Sweetheart, let's go uptown and eat so you won't have to cook."

"No, we'd better not. With two funerals coming up the next couple days, I want to get home and start my dishes for their dinners. I think I'll make cherry pie for one and chicken and dumplings for the other."

"Well, all right. But we could just make a right turn here, eat, then go on home."

"No, I might not have time to finish before church time tonight. Just go on across the road and head for home. Watch out, Ben! Speed up, that car's coming awful fast."

"I can't, I can't, the motor's dead!"

Ben wasn't hurt. But the impact threw Manerva into his arms, her body crushed. Friday, November 19, the doctor came into the hospital waiting room and told Ben and Pauline that Manerva had slipped away.

Ben sobbed. Pauline sat with her children, quietly crying. Marvin and Louise Long were there, comforting them.

After a few moments Ben looked up through tears

and said, "My sweetheart is in the presence of the Lord she loves. And she's enjoying that beautiful mansion He built for her. I'm sure she's already looked up Brother Popejoy and said, 'I told you so.' "

A year and a half after Manerva's death, Ben reached his ninetieth birthday.

"Dad, what do you want for your birthday?" Pauline asked him.

"I don't want anything. I've got all the sweaters, neckties, and socks I'll ever need. There's not one thing I want any of you to buy for me."

"Now, Dad, you know that when a person reaches his ninetieth birthday, it's not going to go unnoticed. And with as many friends and relatives as you've got, we all want to do something special for you."

"I don't want you to spend any money on presents."

"Then what do you want?"

"All right, I'll just tell you. I want to preach. That's all I want. But I'm too old and nobody's going to let me preach now. So you and everybody else just forget all about my birthday."

Later Pauline called Pastor Long and said, "I did what you asked. I spoke to Dad about his birthday."

"What did he say?"

"He said the only thing he wanted was to preach."

"Oh, good! I'm glad he said that. My wife and I discussed it. I wanted to ask him, but she was afraid that with all the other festivities we have planned for him, preaching would be too much. She begged me not to ask him. She's pretty protective of him, you know."

"Yes, I know. I know how all the church love him."

On Sunday, April 1, 1984, one day before his birthday, Ben stood behind a pulpit, his favorite spot, once again addressing a congregation of people who deeply loved him, and, once more, returning that love with all his heart.

Pauline watched as her father stood tall, and listened as he spoke with the same compassionate, tender, booming voice that didn't really need the mike that had been clipped to his tie by Pastor Long.

How sure and comfortable he is standing there! she thought. *Not like his first sermon fifty-eight years ago when he shook with fear and had to hold on to the pulpit to steady himself. He belongs where he is right now. Oh, that he had another ninety years to tell the world of God's love!*

At the close of Ben's sermon, Pastor Long, who is also an executive presbyter of the Northern California and Nevada District, put his arm around Ben's shoulder and said to the congregation of more than four hundred, "The cry of Brother Givens' heart, the call of God, is just as strong today as when he received it. That cry has not changed. This is my spiritual father, he means everything to me.

"Let us enjoy the paths that have been paved for us, and walk in them. Paths that lead to victory and overcoming. Paths that we, as Pentecostal people, will not set aside for anyone."

On May 2, 1984, in San Jose, the Northern California and Nevada District of the Assemblies of God honored ninety-year-old Reverend Benjamin H. Givens for fifty years of dedicated service. He stood straight and tall with tears in his eyes.

Pauline watched from an honored pew. *If only Mother were here now,* she thought. *They made quite a team. Always sharing everything—their ministry, the good times and the bad, and their home—with everyone who came along. Their hearts belonged not only to each other and to me, but to their congregation and relatives as well.*

She remembered many times coming home from school, or wherever she happened to be, and hearing them in their bedroom crying and praying for her, or their families, or their congregation. God gave the Givens the strength of character and the compassion for souls that enabled them to become great prayer warriors and counselors.

But most of all Pauline remembered happy times: laughter and fun, clean jokes and crazy tricks, for everyone. They always had time to play and laugh and love.

Ben and Manerva Givens met with eagerness the challenges that God placed before them. Whether it was facing the prejudices of society, a deeply depressed economy, a world war, or prosperous times, they spread the full gospel story—fearing God, nothing else. Though they began as preachers in the second generation of Pentecostal believers, without the inspiration of a general revival, they could say with Paul, "I have fought a good fight, I have finished my course, I have kept the faith."

Their brush arbors are gone now, but their legacy remains. It is a legacy of sacrificial ministry, a legacy of love, a legacy of the true Pentecostal preacher.

Rev. and Mrs. Benjamin Givens on their 60th wedding anniversary

Epilogue

Ben Givens lives alone in Live Oak, California. After Manerva's death Pauline moved to Live Oak to be near her father. Ben faithfully attends Calvary Temple in Yuba City, California. He is keenly aware of the needs of others. Often when a young person stands behind the pulpit to sing his or her first solo, just when all is very quiet and the music is about to start, Ben's booming voice breaks the silence with, "Lord, bless them nearly to death." The tenseness is broken and the singer relaxes.